ADVANCE PRAISE

"Having spent the majority of my life serving with and leading the brave men and women of our Armed Forces, I learned firsthand the difference between 'average' and 'outstanding.' The difference isn't about who gets knocked down but about who, after going down, gets back up stronger and better for their struggles, failures, or challenges. Ken Falke and Josh Goldberg address the attributes that make our military men and women absolutely remarkable, and provide a road map for growing from the challenges we face."

—GENERAL HUGH SHELTON, US ARMY (RETIRED), 14TH CHAIRMAN OF THE JOINT CHIEFS OF STAFF

"Ken Falke and Josh Goldberg have built a remarkable organization to help those who have faced life's greatest challenges. Their open minds and dedication to innovation have produced Struggle Well, with personal accounts of how they have found ways to transform their own lives. In these stories, readers will find pathways toward their own transformations."

—RICHARD TEDESCHI, PHD, PROFESSOR OF PSYCHOLOGY, UNC CHARLOTTE, AUTHOR OF *THE POSTTRAUMATIC GROWTH WORKBOOK*

"*Struggle Well is a superb account of how two highly respected thought leaders are shifting our view of combat trauma from one of disorder and dysfunction to one of evolution and growth.*"

"*Over the past four years, Ken and Josh have built a world-class program on the conviction that physical and mental trauma can actually present opportunities for personal transformation and growth. With leadership, training, and structure, they encourage, motivate, and inspire the confidence that helps people overcome life's challenges. Struggle Well is innovative, brilliant, and important—and it works.*"

"*At Boulder Crest Retreat, Ken Falke and Josh Goldberg have created a program that is truly revolutionary and effective. Most programs aim to help struggling veterans function in the aftermath of trauma. Boulder Crest is the first program that trains these veterans to grow from their experience, to use their trauma to become better people, and to lead more meaningful lives. Struggle Well, which reflects the authors' deep understanding of this complex problem, is a compelling and engaging read and crucial for anyone who is suffering in the aftermath of trauma.*"

STRUGGLE WELL

Tyler —
Thank you in advance for
what will be an amazing + educational
experience.

Be Well
Do Well
#StruggleWell

STRUGGLE WELL

THRIVING IN THE AFTERMATH OF TRAUMA

KEN FALKE

AND

JOSH GOLDBERG

LIONCREST
PUBLISHING

STRUGGLE WELL
Thriving in the Aftermath of Trauma

ISBN   978-1-5445-1038-5 *Hardcover*
       978-1-5445-1037-8 *Paperback*
       978-1-5445-1036-1 *Ebook*

CONTENTS

FOREWORD

STRUGGLE IS A TERRIBLE
THING TO WASTE

It's not much fun being a prisoner of war for one hour, much less 2,103 days. That's how long I spent as a POW during the Vietnam War, from 1967–1973, living in the ironically named "Hanoi Hilton." The torture, physical and mental anguish, and feelings of loss and abandonment are experiences that no person should ever endure. And while I wouldn't wish six years as a POW on anyone, I have to say these were undoubtedly the years of my life when I grew the strongest and matured the most.

I learned that just because you're in a prison doesn't mean you are a prisoner. My cramped cell measured just eight feet wide by eight feet long—but the real prison was only eight inches wide: the space between my ears.

My challenge, above all, was a mental game.

Through a deep sense of connection with my fellow POWs; the remarkable leadership provided by James Stockdale and others; a renewed sense of faith, confidence, and mission; and a great deal of time in solitude and self-reflection, I was able to endure the experience. More importantly, I was able to use it as fuel to live a life of purpose, service, connection, and growth.

My story of resilience and endurance is not the exception; among the 591 men who returned home with me in 1973, growth was the rule. While over 30 percent of all Vietnam veterans returned home from war dealing with PTSD, only 4 percent of POWs faced similar difficulties.

Perhaps even more remarkable than the 4 percent number is our collective experience since our repatriation; the men who returned home from nine months to ten years in captivity are living fulfilling, service-oriented, and successful lives. Compared to non-POW naval aviators, we report greater satisfaction on every key measure of life.

In 1973, there was no official diagnosis for what we had experienced. This changed in 1995, when Dr. Richard Tedeschi and Dr. Lawrence Calhoun from the University of North Carolina, Charlotte, coined the term "Posttraumatic Growth," or PTG.

Perhaps best explained by Nietzsche, PTG is the experi-

loaded →

ence of allowing what didn't kill you to make you stronger.
This idea that times of deep struggle can cultivate a pro- _deep change_
found and abiding sense of strength and growth is a notion
as old as humankind, and the foundational principle for
nearly every organized religion. Those ancient stories _Are they_
teach us, in combination with more modern ones like _making_
my own, that when we struggle deeply, we are forced to _a religion_
engage in self-reflection and introspection, contemplat-
ing what truly matters in our lives. What often results is
growth in five areas: increased personal strength, deeper
and more meaningful relationships, a greater appreciation
for the small things in life, a richer spiritual or religious
life, and new possibilities for the future.

Big leap

Our nation seems to have lost its way in how we look at
times of great difficulty and struggle. We see it in a thirty- _but_
year high in the suicide rate; rampant opioid, drug, and _neglects_
alcohol abuse and overdoses; a profound sense of discon- _role of_
nection, isolation, and loneliness; and nearly unbelievable _Pharma._
levels of anxiety and depression.

While it is unlikely that you will find yourself as a POW
for six years, all of our lives inevitably feature ups and
downs. The question is, how can we ensure that we enjoy
the good times, and wring every ounce of value, strength,
and growth out of the bad ones?

Two years ago, I met Ken Falke and Josh Goldberg. We

spoke in depth about this very challenge, along with the work they were undertaking at Boulder Crest in Virginia. Through a comprehensive understanding of PTG, collaboration with Dr. Tedeschi, a deep regard for understanding the stories of PTG in action—such as in the Hanoi Hilton—and training expertise, these two men had pioneered a profound breakthrough. They had figured out how to cultivate and facilitate PTG in combat veterans who had served in Iraq and Afghanistan. Ken, Josh, and their incredible team at Boulder Crest has enabled people to take what didn't kill them and use that experience to make them far stronger and more fulfilled than they ever thought possible.

With the progress they have made, there was only one thing left to do: expand their reach to the millions of people in our nation—both veterans and civilians—who are struggling to make sense of their own challenges, seeking to find their way to a great and purposeful life.

This book, capturing all that Ken and Josh have learned along the way, represents a roadmap to ensure that anyone can harness the age-old power of struggle, and not simply survive but thrive.

Never forget: we only get so many struggles in life. It's a terrible thing to waste any of them.

—CAPTAIN CHARLIE PLUMB, (RET.) US NAVY

 *Captain Charlie Plumb has lived what he believes to be the American Dream. As a farm kid from Kansas, he fantasized about airplanes, although he felt certain he would never have the opportunity to pilot one. It would be the United States Navy that afforded Plumb the opportunity to live out that dream.*

After graduating from the Naval Academy, Plumb completed Navy Flight Training and reported to Miramar Naval Air Station in San Diego, where he flew the first adversarial flights in the development of what would be called The Navy Fighter Weapons School, currently known as "TOP GUN." The next year, Plumb's squadron, The Aardvarks launched on the Aircraft Carrier USS Kitty Hawk with Fighter Squadron 114 to fly the Navy's hottest airplane, the F-4 Phantom Jet. Code named "Plumber," Charlie Plumb flew seventy-four successful combat missions over North Vietnam and made over one hundred carrier landings. On his seventy-fifth mission, just five days before the end of his tour, Plumb was shot down over Hanoi, taken prisoner, tortured, and spent the next 2,103 $\underline{Years}$ days as a Prisoner of War.

Following his repatriation, Plumb continued his Navy flying career in Reserve Squadrons where he flew A-4 Skyhawks, A-7 Corsairs, and FA-18 Hornets. His last two commands as a

Naval Reservist were on the Aircraft Carrier Coral Sea and at a Fighter Air Wing in California. He retired from the United States Navy after thirty-one years of service.

To this day, Captain Plumb continues to fly left-seat at every opportunity. He has personally owned eight airplanes, the most treasured being a World War II PT-19 Open-Cockpit Antique. He currently flies the PT-19 and his Rutan-designed experimental single-engine Long-Ez. His autobiography, I'm No Hero, *is in its thirty-second printing. For more information, go to: www.CharliePlumb.com.*

INTRODUCTION

"What works for PTSD, anxiety, and depression? Nothing. Nothing is working." ... Uh.

—LEADING PSYCHIATRIST

If you've picked up this book, we are assuming one thing: things are bad. Why else would the title *Struggle Well* grab your attention?

We've been there. And we have engaged with and guided thousands of others who have been there too. In fact, that's why we feel confident making what might seem like a laughable claim to someone who is seriously struggling: struggle can produce profound gifts, if you can learn to struggle well. Because we've experienced personally just how hard it is to struggle badly, we feel passionate about offering you, our reader, a roadmap to help you move forward. We want you to have the kind of support and guidance we wish we'd had during our struggles.

The seven chapters following this Introduction take you through this journey, step by step. These steps are documented in research and proven in the real world. For years, we have seen profound healing and growth in the veterans and military family members who came to us with Posttraumatic Stress Disorder (PTSD). We know this stuff works because we've watched the proof play out.

We'll also share some of our own stories along the way to illustrate our points. As we explain in some of the subsequent chapters, sharing your story is a key step in moving beyond some of the harmful byproducts of struggle—like depression, anxiety, and PTSD—and moving forward to achieve Posttraumatic Growth (PTG). We also believe that sharing openly is an important step in building trust—and if you're going to put any of these steps into practice, we assume you'd like to trust us.

This book is more than a collection of stories and practices though. You don't learn by only seeing how others have turned struggle into strength—you learn by doing it yourself. The final component of this book, therefore, involves you doing the work. We've provided sections throughout the chapters for you to apply some of the steps we talk about. If taken seriously, applying these steps can produce transformative life change.

The work we do started as a result of Ken's experiences,

so we'll start by focusing on his story; we'll also provide a big-picture understanding of what this book is about. Josh picks up the narration when we get to his story in Chapter One.

KEN: MY STORY

My story is one of a search for purpose and meaning, something I eventually found in the US Navy. On my way to a successful career, I dealt with loss and disappointment, but I fought against letting those experiences define me. At this point in my life, I've also seen plenty of people who have endured trauma. Some of those people have learned to thrive in spite of the hits they've taken—and they helped lead me to the work I'm doing now, helping people achieve Posttraumatic Growth.

My mother died of cancer when I was seven years old. She was just twenty-nine, and she was in a coma for a year before she died. My mother's death changed our family dramatically. My father was an Army veteran and a policeman in Washington, DC. Now he had two small boys to raise—me, and my then four-year-old brother. My dad remarried a couple years after my mother died, and my new stepmother had two children, including a boy my age who became my childhood best friend. We were a loving family, and like all teenage kids, I was looking for something bigger and better in my life. I spent my summers shuttling between Washington, DC and Pittsburgh, playing ice hockey and spending time with my grandparents. Unfortunately, my grandfather was an abusive alcoholic. I would drown out the noise of his fights with my drug-addicted uncle by sleeping with a pillow over my head and opening up a window to let in the loud noise of the nearby Pennsylvania Turnpike.

After barely graduating high school, I left home to play on a professional hockey team in Texas. I was a great player, but I was by far the smallest guy there and knew I wasn't going to make the cut. I wanted to do something different with my life, and the military seemed the obvious solution. My childhood mentors, including my scoutmasters, teachers, and coaches, were all military officers who served in Vietnam, and I had close childhood friends whose dads were military officers. Those were the "good guys" in my life and I liked the idea of being a good guy.

I joined the Navy at age nineteen and spent most of my twenty-one years of service as an explosive ordnance disposal (EOD) technician. During that time, I made over one thousand parachute jumps, about the same number of underwater dives, and blew up hundreds of thousands of pounds of explosive devices. I led men and women on some incredibly challenging missions.

In March of 1989, at twenty-seven years of age, I was

severely injured in a parachuting accident in Puerto *(ow)* Rico. I fractured my two lowest vertebrae, dislocated my shoulder, and had my fourth major concussion. I was dragged down the runway by high winds and lost a large amount of skin off my arm. I thought that was the end of my career—and maybe the end of my life. But thanks to good care and strong personal motivation, I went on to complete twenty-one years of honorable service.

After eighteen years in the Navy, I hit the highest enlisted rank, and I knew there was nowhere else to go. Sitting at a desk wasn't for me; I was happiest when I was in a rubber boat or jumping out of planes. It was time to leave and pursue meaningful work somewhere else.

I retired in 2002 and started a consulting company, looking at different technologies to help improve the fight against terrorism. We employed about fifty Special Forces guys and bomb disposal experts who were focused on weapons *?* of mass destruction. I'd just returned from a trip overseas when the first bomb went off in Iraq, killing four Soldiers in an unarmored Humvee. Almost immediately, there was huge demand for the work we were doing.

Profiting off of war crimes nice.

Within eighteen months of this first major bombing incident in Iraq, our company grew from fifty to nearly five hundred employees, and people started approaching me about selling the company. I found some private equity investors to help continue the business' growth, and sold them the majority of the company. I stayed with the business and ran it for a couple more years before finally deciding to leave.

At that point, I sensed the new direction I wanted to take my life, and it involved helping military veterans. For the previous six years, I had spent time visiting wounded EOD technicians in the hospital. That started in 2004, when I received a call from a friend serving in Iraq. One of his Soldiers had lost both legs in a roadside bomb incident, and he asked me to meet the young man at a hospital in Washington, DC. When I got to the hospital, there was no family there. The young man explained to me that all he had was his mom, and she had no money. She couldn't get to DC to be next to her son who'd lost both legs.

My wife, Julia, and I paid for his mom to come to Washington to be with her son. It wasn't a big expense and, truthfully, I thought the war would be over in three or four months and he would be the first and only guy that we saw lose his legs. Boy, was I wrong. As I write this, more than 225 men and women, all skilled EOD technicians, have lost limbs, been blinded, paralyzed, or severely burned.[1] One young man lost all four limbs. Our small EOD community has lost 133 lives on today's battlefield and almost this same number to suicide.[2]

I ended up spending years visiting wounded servicemen and women, and Julia and I founded the EOD Warrior Foundation in 2007, which supports wounded EOD technicians and provides for the families of those who have been killed in action or died by suicide. We began inviting these hospitalized EOD families for meals and short stays at our home in the Blue Ridge Mountains of Virginia. Eventually, we were inspired to make a sustained commitment to the veteran community through building Boulder Crest Retreat Virginia, the first private wellness center in the country serving active duty military, reserves, National Guard personnel, veterans, first responders, their family members, and Gold Star families.

Throughout this time, I began to notice something that puzzled me. The guys who seemed to struggle most weren't the people I expected. I met with dozens of people who had lost multiple limbs, including Taylor Morris, a quadruple amputee. A guy like this would be my pick for someone who went on to struggle with PTSD, but Taylor wasn't. In the hospital, up on his whiteboard, Taylor had his goals: "Today, I'm going to learn how to put on my own prosthetic arm and eat a brownie without crushing it. Tomorrow, I'm going to walk ten laps on my new prosthetic legs." He was sitting in bed and determinedly working on his goals. I was inspired by his attitude, drive, and his progress.

Then I started seeing guys with Posttraumatic Stress Disorder (PTSD) coming to the Retreat. They didn't have physical injuries, but they weren't doing as well mentally as amputees like Taylor. I thought, "How can you lose four limbs and not have PTSD?" These Soldiers have seen the same grief and distress on the battlefield as one another, but this other guy comes back without physical injuries and struggles to function in life. I began thinking about that.

One day, a Soldier's wife said to me, "I wish my husband had lost his legs. At least people would know what's wrong with him." My reaction was, "That's a horrible thing to say. The last thing you want is to lose your legs. What IS wrong with your husband?"

"He's got PTSD," she answered. I replied, "That's fine. We can work with him, and we can help make his and your life better."

At that point, our work started to take a turn toward the PTSD community. I began searching for research about how to instill a deep and abiding sense of strength and personal growth in veterans with PTSD. That search led me to the work of Dr. Richard G. Tedeschi and Dr. Lawrence G. Calhoun, who pioneered research in the field of Posttraumatic Growth (PTG).

But before I found Tedeschi and Calhoun's work on

Posttraumatic Growth, I encountered a lot of ineffective programs.

WHAT'S NOT WORKING

When we opened Boulder Crest Retreat Virginia, we recognized that the families we were serving needed something beyond a comfortable place to stay. There were plenty of nonprofit organizations out there with programs helping veterans, so we started inviting the organizations to use our retreat center for free, hoping they'd be able to offer needed help to the families we were hosting. But the programs were a mixed bag. Some of them were good, but some of them were terrible. Most of them were somewhere in the middle of the road.

For the most part, none of what they were doing was documented in a curriculum that could scale and solve the problem. They had some evidence to prove why it worked and how it worked, but I didn't see a clear path on how it could solve the mental health crisis in our combat veterans. That bothered me.

I had spent two of my Navy tours as an instructor and curriculum developer. My company had trained 50,000 Soldiers a year to do one of the most sophisticated tasks on the battlefield—finding and disarming improvised explosive devices (IEDs)—so I had some experience taking a program to scale. I knew we needed to create a standardized curriculum for PTSD. It can't be all about one person who thinks he can magically cure another. That's not the way life works, and it's not the way healing works.

In the bomb disposal fight in Iraq and Afghanistan, our goal was always to figure out how to solve the problem. We'll never stop people from using bombs, but we taught our troops how to find them and how to find those who were building and placing them. Now, at the retreat, I had to once again help solve a problem.

In the process of searching for a program that would work, I met Josh Goldberg (co-author of this book) when he showed up at one of our retreats; he'll tell that story in Chapter One. In December 2013, we had our first extended discussion on the topic of PTSD and struggle. The session lasted for eight hours at my dining room table, and we bonded over our shared objective: we were not interested in helping one veteran, or thirty, or even three hundred. We were willing to dedicate the remainders of our lives and every ounce of effort and energy we had if, and only if, we could work toward fundamentally solving the problems of anxiety, depression, PTSD, and suicide. To accomplish that, we had to create a transformational and scalable solution.

TAKING OUR PROGRAMS TO SCALE

To help veterans sustain the progress made at our retreats, and to scale our efforts to a broader population, we had to figure out why current mental health programs for veterans with PTSD weren't working, and find ones that did.

We were able to identify some significant problems in the programs being offered to veterans. First, we recognized that many people who get into the mental health field are themselves dealing with some significant mental health issues. They do this work in hopes that helping others will help themselves. We saw plenty of unhealthy mental health providers offering programs intended to help, but their own issues made them at best unhelpful, and at worst, counterproductive.

Combat veterans, in particular, are trained to look for high threats and risks on the battlefield. They see right through someone who is pretending to be well—in the military, we sum this up by saying, "Bullshit is transparent." In addition, a RAND Corporation survey confirmed that many community mental health providers aren't adequately trained to understand military culture.[3] This often results in a lack of fit between therapist and veteran, causing the veteran to drop out of treatment.

Second, none of the programs we hosted had any ability

to scale. When we asked the people offering their services to "scale up," they adjusted their programs to accommodate thirty people rather than twenty. But then they couldn't provide the one-on-one time that people needed to really get better. Instead, they had six providers and thirty participants, and twenty-four of the participants were sitting behind the six that were getting the majority of the attention. This is no way to scale.

Another problem we identified was that most of the programs we saw were what we call "catch and release." That means you go to a retreat, you have a great week, and after that we're done with you; you're on your own. We have to bring in the next thirty participants. People experienced a temporary "high" while at the retreat, but once they returned home, they were back where they started. There was no lasting change or healing.

Finally, we recognized that many programs, especially on the clinical treatment side, were largely about symptom management. The focus of these approaches is on determining a diagnosis and using a combination of drugs and talk therapy to help someone feel less bad, rather than offering a proactive approach about how to struggle well and grow. Ultimately, that symptom-management approach seemed to set veterans and their families up for never-ending need; they would always be reliant on some sort of help to function that would likely include a

Some people need meds

fistful of pills with nasty side effects. We wanted to equip people to learn how to thrive on their own.

Ultimately, the million-dollar question became, "How do we sustain the benefits of a short-duration, high-impact retreat?"

I went all kinds of places looking for answers—Harvard, the University of San Francisco, the University of Chicago, the Palo Alto Department of Veterans Affairs (VA), and a program in Napa Valley called The Pathway Home. I went to the University of Southern California in Los Angeles and spoke to two doctors at San Diego State University. I met with a life coach from California and another from Colorado. We met with the head of mental health at the VA, and we heard over and over again that the system to address PTSD doesn't work.

I asked a psychiatrist in San Francisco, "If these treatments don't work for combat veterans, why do you use them?" He said, "They're all we have, and all that's approved for use and reimbursement by the insurance companies." To me, it's unacceptable to keep delivering the same program and expect different results. As a bomb disposal guy, you really can't make these kinds of mistakes; if you do, you'll probably only make them once.

Wicked Problem

The search for answers led me to Drs. Richard G. Tedeschi and Lawrence G. Calhoun at the University of North Carolina, Charlotte. Before I met Rich, I was starting to feel hopeless; there was no indication I'd find positive outcomes for either the practitioners or the people we were serving. But Tedeschi spoke about hope. He emphasized that people could find meaning, purpose, and significance, even out of the worst tragedies.

Tedeschi and Calhoun had spent more than thirty years studying people's ability to recover from tragedy and trauma. They interviewed parents who had lost children, primarily to cancer, and found that these families often emerged from their experience a much better version of themselves. They found new meaning and purpose in life. Their family relationships grew stronger, and they found ways to help others. These parents would have traded all this newfound wisdom to have their children back, but they acknowledged the positives that had come from their loss. Tedeschi and Calhoun coined the term "Posttraumatic Growth" (PTG) to explain this phenomenon.[4]

When I met Rich, I said, "I understand your framework. I know you've researched it, and you've seen that PTG is possible. But can you teach someone how to achieve it?" At first, Rich didn't understand the question. When we told him more about what we do at Boulder Crest, he was intrigued and offered to help.

We enlisted Rich's services, and we started tweaking our program based on his feedback. Rich and another one of his colleagues, Dr. Bret Moore—a former US Army psychologist who deployed to Iraq twice—sat through our program, and we revised the curriculum again and again until we felt we got it right. The result? We're ready to share it with you over the next seven chapters.

LEARNING TO STRUGGLE WELL

PTSD shouldn't be a disorder that follows you around for the rest of your life.

Here's how I describe PTSD. Imagine you've saved all your money to buy your dream car, a beautiful red Ferrari. You go to the dealer and pay half a million dollars cash to buy it. You sit in the seat, put your foot on the brake, push the start button, and the engine roars. You've never been happier; you've achieved the vision of what you want your life to be. But when you drive out of the dealership, you drive all the way home going ten miles an hour, staring in the rearview mirror. That's PTSD.

As any good driver knows, you have to look in your rearview and side mirrors to know what's around you and behind you—but you cannot stare!

You lost your legs to an IED in Afghanistan. You can't get them back. But you can't let what happened define you.

Here's the truth. Your red Ferrari goes two hundred miles an hour. It's got a windshield that's five feet wide and three feet tall, big enough to show you the bright future you're headed toward. If you put your foot to the pedal and look out that windshield, you can go! You need to learn how to live in the present while sitting in the driver's seat and look forward to achieve Posttraumatic Growth.

Damn.

When we diagnose people, or give them labels, or call out every single symptom—and give people a pill for every problem—they take their foot off the gas. They remain stuck in hopelessness and despair. They become diminished versions of themselves.

This is not what people want, no matter how difficult their lives are. People want fulfillment and connection. They want purpose and progress. They want growth, love, and peace. When we treat people as if we believe this is possible, *it becomes possible.*

Making PTG happen begins with understanding that everyone struggles. Bad things happen, but what distinguishes the people who grow and prosper is the fact that they're not afraid to struggle. They embrace struggle because they know it's inevitable and even useful. Struggle can help us achieve the life we want to live.

THE ROAD AHEAD

We've learned in working with veterans that their problems have a lot more to do with what they are coming home to, rather than what they are coming back from. The military teaches men and women how to be Soldiers, but no one teaches them how to live a meaningful and productive life out of uniform. In truth, no one teaches civilians how to do that either—until now.

Here's why we think that's so important. In our work with veterans, it's not unusual to talk to someone who has seen hundreds of dead bodies lying around. Those experiences leave a mark. Yet when we started listening to the people coming through our program, few, if any, of the stories were solely about combat. All of their stories kept going back to what happened before they joined the military: being physically, mentally, or sexually abused as a child or having alcoholic or drug-addicted parents. Research calls experiences like these Adverse Childhood Experiences (ACEs). If trauma from childhood explains the suicide epidemic, and rampant anxiety, depression, and PTSD amongst the veteran community, it stands to reason that the same is true for their civilian counterparts.

The good news is that if the experience of trauma is nearly universal, so, too, is the potential for Posttraumatic Growth. Our work is appropriate for anyone who is struggling. In fact, it's not about the trauma itself. The more we think of ourselves as "victims" of this, or "survivors" of that, the more we limit our possibilities and become trapped as a *diminished version of ourselves*. When we label our symptoms as "PTSD," "moral injury," "military sexual trauma," "survivors' guilt," "anxiety," or "depression," and relive the negative events we've experienced, that label becomes the dominant narrative in our lives.

PTG teaches us that it's what we choose to learn from our struggle that matters. Let's face it—life is going to slap you in the face, maybe even punch you. You can choose to *react* negatively, or you can choose to *respond* positively, turning your struggle into strength.

Drawing on our experiences with veterans, we'll teach you how to "take a knee"—to empty your heavy backpack of the pain, fear, shame, and disappointment you've been carrying. If someone has given you a "label" or diagnosis, put it down while you read this book. Labels only hold you back.

At the heart of this book is our deeply held conviction that *everyone struggles in life, and everyone can learn to struggle well*. We believe that struggle is inevitable, inherently valuable, and useful in creating the life you desire. We see this daily in our work and we're proud to make this available to anyone who needs it—which is everyone!

In the pages that follow, we provide a road map for transforming struggle into strength. We explain why struggle is important and outline the five domains and five phases of PTG. We share practices for optimal wellness and explore what goes wrong when we feed our depression and anxiety in unhealthy ways. We provide practices that allow you to make peace with your past, live in the present, and create the great future you deserve. With a new perspective and healthy habits, you'll be able to create and live your new story.

One of the most well-known military slogans is, "Be all that you can be." This Army slogan is an invitation to step into the service. The road map for PTG that we provide in this book is designed to help you "be all that you can be" wherever you are in life, in or out of uniform. Let's start Chapter One by discussing the inevitability and importance of struggle.

CHAPTER ONE

STRUGGLE IS A TERRIBLE THING TO WASTE

—

"It is by going down into the abyss that we recover the treasures of life."[5]

—JOSEPH CAMPBELL

Everything you need to have the life you want is within you. The key is to figure out how to access it. In this chapter, we'll begin to show you why it's important to dig deep.

We reveal how struggle forces you to look into the abyss. We show you what steps you need to take to walk the road from struggle to strength. We reveal the innumerable treasures you'll collect along the way. We also share Josh's story with you, because by disclosing our struggles, we remove the barriers that keep us from connecting deeply to one another and helping each other grow.

OPPORTUNITIES FROM STRUGGLE

We believe that struggle is both inevitable and useful. That doesn't make us masochists; it makes us realists. We're not suggesting that struggle or trauma are good—only that they happen in everyone's life.

We believe struggle is useful because it forces you to take a knee and reflect on what's true about yourself and about the world. Trauma—whether it involves being physically, sexually, or emotionally abused; wounded on the battle-field; or imprisoned—has real physiological effects. You may have difficulty sleeping and become anxious and depressed. You may be easily triggered by sights, sounds, or smells that cause you to relive a traumatic event.

But trauma involves more than what happens to your body. Trauma, especially when it is repeated and prolonged, shatters your core beliefs about yourself and the world. Suddenly, the way in which you interpreted the world no longer makes sense.

When you are exposed to trauma that you have no way to process, it's as if you are trying to navigate the world with a broken compass. You don't know which way is up, and you find yourself stuck or lost. Your sense of safety and of self are destroyed. You believed you could handle anything. You thought the world was fair and safe, but then something happened that disproved those assumptions. What you're left with is a broken view of the world.

At face value this sounds bad. Yet when you accept struggle rather than fight it, you have an unprecedented opportunity to look deep within yourself. You have a chance to examine your beliefs, how you arrived at your view of the world, and what's genuinely true for you. From there, you get to build a life that's authentic, fulfilling, and purposeful—a life that might not have been possible any other way.

You have to be willing to look deep within yourself—to stare into the abyss—to find the answers you seek. When you accept struggle, you stop searching outside yourself for answers. You stop looking to other people. You stop using drugs or alcohol, spending money you don't have, or overeating. When you stop looking outside yourself, you begin the journey inward to figure out what's true and what resonates deep within you.

Posttraumatic Growth gives you the opportunity to claim a new label—a label that proclaims that you've been through really difficult times and you didn't simply survive, you thrived. You thrived not in spite of, but because of your experiences.

Many people don't know that there's a way through struggle that doesn't include self-medicating or unhealthy coping mechanisms. They are wandering in the darkness because no one has told them that light exists. We believe the greatest human yearning is to continue to grow and evolve to be a better version of ourselves, each and every day. If you offer people that path, the vast majority of them choose it.

AN "EPIDEMIC OF HOPE"

An epidemic of hopelessness is causing society's major ills, including overdose deaths, homelessness, and suicide. We believe we need an "epidemic of hope," and struggle can provide that. This idea that struggle has inherent value and can help you create the life you seek is not new; it can be found in writings as old as the ancient scriptures.

"We also glory in our sufferings, because we know that suffering produces perseverance; perseverance, character; and character, hope."

—ROMANS 5:3-5

If struggle is this powerful and produces such good, why don't more people recognize its value? And why aren't more people embracing it?

In part, as we've noted, it's because no one has shown

them there's a better way. But it's also true that even when struggle forces you into the abyss, you may not want to go there. You may be afraid to examine your life—especially if you have no one to guide you—for fear of what you might find. This was certainly true for Josh, as he explains below, but it was by being forced to explore the abyss within himself that he was finally able to find freedom from pain and suffering.

JOSH'S STORY: INTO THE ABYSS

On the surface, I had the perfect life. I excelled in school, married well, and had a beautiful home. I was a successful executive for a major oil company with not one, but two corner offices, and I traveled the world. I was respected and well-liked.

I had everything I ever sought to have, which was money, power, and respect—and yet, I felt profoundly unhappy. In 2011, my wife asked me a work-related question that would prove to be life-altering: "Is this what you want to do for the rest of your life?" I didn't know how to respond, so I spent a lot of time reflecting on my answer.

I began with a personal analysis. I evaluated what I was good at, what I wasn't good at, my opportunities, and the areas that truly interested me. I initiated conversations with people who seemed incredibly fulfilled. It began as a networking effort—I sat with probably fifty people and asked, "How did you get here?" I heard stories of struggle, stories of triumph, stories of delight, and stories of purpose. Repeatedly, I heard that they couldn't tell the difference between their work and their lives; they simply loved getting up every morning.

"Every man takes the limits of his own field of vision for the limits of the world."[6]

—ARTHUR SCHOPENHAUER

For the first time, I saw my own limited vision. The people I was meeting had a sense of peace, purpose, joy, and fulfillment that I'd never seen before. They made me realize what was possible.

At that point, I said to myself, "That's what I want."

The first obvious step to me seemed to require moving away from the false life I'd built. Over the course of six months, I made huge changes. I switched careers and built new habits. The falseness had permeated my relationships as well—even my closest ones. The people who liked and loved me were attached to a person I didn't want to be. I found a new group of friends, and most difficult of all, got divorced. All of this was liberating in many respects, but also incredibly frightening and destabilizing. I knew how to step away from what I didn't want, but had no idea how to get to where I wanted to go. I felt trapped in a deep, deep darkness.

I was overwhelmed by things that I had ignored or repressed. I suffered from severe insomnia for ten years, dating back to my senior year of college. I was sleeping about one to two hours a night, if I was lucky. I regularly experienced severe anxiety and panic attacks; I felt constantly afraid and plagued with doubt and guilt. On Thanksgiving Day in 2012, I sat with my family and friends around a feast-laden table, and when we were prompted to share what we were thankful for, I couldn't think of a single thing.

All of this caught up with me and overtook me like a tidal wave. For the first part of 2013, I experienced severe panic attacks, regularly had suicidal thoughts, and developed a plan to take my life.

To add insult to injury, my work was unfulfilling, and my mother's cancer had spread to her head. I went to a therapist, who turned out to be incredibly cruel, at a point when I was at my most vulnerable. I found another therapist, who was equally unhelpful but fortunately a bit kinder, and I ended up sitting in a room one or two times a week, talking to myself. That turned out to be a wonderful opportunity for me to engage in introspection and self-exploration.

Still, I lacked any meaningful practices to manage and learn from my struggle. Instead, I was given anti-anxiety pills, anti-depressants, and sleeping pills, which allowed me to get some sleep and be a bit calmer, but didn't do anything to solve the root causes of my problem. I took a trip around the world—thirteen countries in three months—that some of my friends labeled Josh's attempt at *Eat-Pray-Love*. It was inspirational and exciting, and I did in fact Eat, Pray, and Love. Yet, when I returned home, there sat everything I was running away from.

I felt liberated by taking off a mask that, for many years, I had no idea I was wearing. But when I had to confront what was under it, I couldn't face myself. I didn't look in the mirror for nearly two years. I bought one of those mirrors that allowed me to shave in the shower so I didn't have to look myself in the eyes.

In the midst of my struggle, I had one positive inclination, and that was to serve a cause greater than my own. As a favor to a friend of my brother's, I agreed to meet with a woman who had lost her brother in Afghanistan. Up to that point, I'd had no contact with the military or veteran communities. So, I started studying everything I could about the challenges veterans face. I read about barriers to employment, education, and health care. I learned about PTSD and suicide; to my surprise, I began recognizing myself in some of the stories I read. After thirty-five years of not having anything to do with the military, I started meeting more and more veterans.

In the process, however, I was called out. I remember one interaction in particular with Dusty, a former Army weightlifting champion and Airborne Ranger. He looked like a modern-day Spartan, with a formidable white goatee, arms as wide as my torso, and profound clarity in his eyes. After talking with Dusty for a while, I explained my purpose in being there: to serve. Dusty looked at me and said, "You seem like a fine young man. Someone who wants to help and has the ability to do so. But before you try to do anything for a single one of my brothers and sisters, you need to do something."

I asked him, "What? What do I need to do?"

Looking deep into my soul with his clear eyes, he replied, "Unfuck yourself."

Soldiers can see hypocrisy from a mile away. Their message, first articulated so concisely by Dusty, was clear: I didn't get to help anyone else get well until I got well. The military community accepts as a given that you have to pay your dues. Growth comes through a disciplined process of learning, training, and growing. They recognize that hard work is a requirement, and that there aren't shortcuts. I wanted an easy way to healing; they reminded me that the *only* way was to start by getting myself right.

In the company of these Soldiers, I was forced to look at myself deeply by people who had strength. I learned about the importance of principles, wellness practices, and a strong support network. Dusty taught me meditation. I came face-to-face with my considerable fear and anxiety, and came to understand how my own training and experiences—from childhood and beyond—had shaped me, both positively and negatively. These battle-tested Warriors supported, nurtured, and guided me, and ultimately helped me find the courage to explore who I truly am in the depths of my spirit and soul.

Veterans saved my life. They taught me how to be a man, how to be strong, how to be a leader, and how to be a person of integrity. For me, understanding that my struggle could lead to growth was powerful. Finding a community and feeling that I belonged were gifts veterans gave me.

I met Ken after Boulder Crest opened in September of 2013, and Ken had set out to learn more about why it was that certain people thrive after war and others don't. As he described in the Introduction, he hosted a number of nonprofit programs focused on PTSD, including one I had become involved with in California. Ken came to visit us, but I had laryngitis that day and couldn't speak (a rare predicament for me, <u>as I love to talk</u>). That forced me to listen and really understand what he was trying to do.

I went to see Ken in Virginia a month later and we built a relationship based on the belief that the challenge of PTSD is solvable. We are both described as contrarians—we don't accept conventional wisdom. We've had widely different life experiences, yet we share a strong sense of the importance of struggle and what it takes to be successful in life. We understand the potential for people to change and grow. It has been the honor of a lifetime to join Ken in this work.

My time with veterans and working with Ken enabled me to finally listen to myself. For the first time in my life, I understood what I wanted to do, not what others thought I should do. I discovered a profound sense of purpose and connection, and a deep understanding of who I am. All of this was only possible because I embraced my struggle and was willing to take the frightening and rewarding journey into my abyss.

From being an inch away from taking my own life, I now find myself waking up every morning with a sense of zeal and zest, joy and purpose. I have an inherent sense of gratitude that this journey is possible.

But I know there are countless others who walk in the

shadows—people who wear their masks, pretend to be okay, and don't have the freedom or ability to share their struggle. What I hope to do through our work and this book is to let each of you, my fellow travelers, know that a great, fulfilling, and amazing life is possible. Paradoxically, you must be willing to go through the despair, the abyss, the challenge, and the struggle to achieve it. My hope is to prevent you from falling as far as I did before you see the light.

POSTTRAUMATIC GROWTH IS REAL AND REPLICABLE

We have witnessed the possibility of PTG in our own lives and in our work at Boulder Crest. Recently, we hosted a mother who had lost her son to suicide. Every year, she organizes a five-kilometer race in the Pacific Northwest that raises hundreds of thousands of dollars to support nonprofits that help prevent suicide. She never would have done that if her son hadn't died.

She would cheerfully hang up her running shoes tomorrow if she could have her son back, but she recognizes that she can't turn back the clock. She continues to move forward, one step at a time, and has created a new life she never could have imagined. This is what Drs. Tedeschi and Calhoun kept seeing over and over again with bereaved parents.

Interestingly, Rich told us that he and Calhoun initially

set out to study people who possessed wisdom. What they found is that the people who possess true wisdom are those who have suffered—whether bereaved parents, people with severe disabilities, or Prisoners of War. As they listened to the voices of those who had experienced traumatic events and had come out wiser on the other side, Tedeschi and Calhoun discovered five specific domains in which they saw growth. These are the treasures you collect in your abyss.

FIVE DOMAINS OF GROWTH: FINDING TREASURES IN THE ABYSS

The first domain of growth is **deeper relationships**. When you struggle, you have a far greater sense of compassion for, and empathy with, other people who struggle; you have a greater sense of kindness for people in general. Your relationships become deeper and more meaningful because you're more authentic and less concerned about being judged.

Personal strength is the second domain of growth. When you have been through a traumatic event and not only survived, but thrived, you understand that you can get through anything. You recognize that you are stronger than you know, and it's only when you're tested that you experience your own strength for what it truly is.

The third domain of growth is **spiritual and existential**

change. When you have a brush with death, thoughts of suicide, or any experience that makes you realize the life you have isn't the life you want, you are forced to reflect on the deepest questions imaginable: "Who am I?" "Why am I here?" "Where do I belong?" You get the opportunity to use your pursuit of the answers to change your life.

A **sense of appreciation for life** is the fourth domain of growth. You come to appreciate the ability to simply breathe. You feel grateful to wake up every day, to spend time with good friends, to watch sunsets, and to do fulfilling work.

The final domain of growth is about **new possibilities**. When you struggle, the path that you were traveling is often no longer available. Now you have the opportunity, and the obligation, to find a new path. Along that road, you are introduced to new ways of living, new people who enrich your life, and new ways of doing things.

Deeper relationships, personal strength, spiritual and existential change, appreciation for life, and new possibilities: these are treasures you collect as you walk the road from struggle to strength. They represent wisdom. They are what life is all about.

FIVE PHASES OF PTG: A LIFELONG PROCESS

It's wonderful to recognize the ways in which people grow, but it's perhaps even more important to understand *how* to get there. Working closely with people who traveled the road from struggle to strength, Tedeschi and Calhoun began to identify a framework and a process by which PTG occurs. No one has tried to operationalize this process, until now. These five phases of PTG are what we teach in our programs with military members, veterans, and their families, and what we teach you in the chapters that follow.

The first phase of PTG is **education**. Knowledge is power *and* liberation. Knowledge allows you to have the keys to your own kingdom. You have to understand three things that we'll talk about in this book: first, the impact that struggle has on your mind, your body, your heart, and your spirit. You need to recognize the physiological and psychological impacts of struggle so you can identify the signals that mean you are growing through them.

Second, you need to recognize and accept that struggle is both inevitable and useful, and that there is a great deal to be gained from pain and distress.

And, third, you need to understand how to struggle well and live well.

Regulation is the second phase of PTG. This involves

finding wellness practices to keep you grounded and well. Practices are not the same as tools that you pick up only when you need them. Practices are those things you actively do on a consistent basis that allow you to connect your head and your heart, and calm your mind and your body. You may have been using unhealthy habits to escape your struggle, such as drinking heavily or using drugs. But even if they seem to help in the short term, these destructive habits make the situation worse.

Healthy practices like meditation, exercise, or taking a walk allow you to feel a sense of calmness, stability, and strength. When you hear people say, "I go to the gym to clear my head," or "I play guitar to empty my mind," they are using practices to help regulate their body and their emotions. We'll discuss regulation more in Chapter Two.

Disclosure, the third phase of PTG is hard work. As you travel through life, you put on a metaphorical rucksack and collect experiences in it. Some of the experiences are good and some are bad, but all of them go into the pack. You may feel you have no control over what goes in, and no ability to take anything out. Eventually, you don't even realize you're carrying around all of these experiences, and you don't take time to examine them to understand what impact they have on you.

Disclosure is about emptying your rucksack because it's

become too heavy to carry. You have to figure out what's in there, share that with others you trust, and decide what you want to put back in. Ultimately, disclosure becomes about living an authentic existence. It's about not being afraid to share what has happened to you during your life, the things you did and didn't do, and not carrying the guilt and shame with you anymore. Disclosure is covered more fully in Chapter Four.

The fourth phase of PTG is the **positive new story** you get to create! What you carry with you going forward helps shape that story. You, and only you, get to decide what to carry in your backpack. You, and only you, get to create a positive story about your future: a story that speaks to who you are, why you exist, where you are going, and who is joining you for the journey. We focus on your new story in Chapter Five.

Service is the fifth and final phase of PTG. Throughout history, the people we look up to—whether that's Martin Luther King, Jr, Mr. Rogers, or Jesus—are people who believed that life is about what you do for others. Service is the focus of Chapter Six.

Often, we define service to mean grand acts and gestures. Yet one of the greatest acts of service we can perform for another human being is the sheer act of listening. Listening deeply allows the other person to be honest and share their story with you. Listening well requires that you set aside all other distractions, suspend judgment, get present, and ask probing and respectful questions, rather than offer advice. In turn, listening to someone else's story liberates you to set down your pack and share your story with them.

Education, regulation, disclosure, a positive new story, and service: these five phases of PTG allow you to walk the road from struggle to strength. They are the foundation for what we teach in person and what we are sharing with you, for the first time, in the pages of this book.

It's important to note that PTG is not a linear or mechanistic process—you don't begin at phase one and end up at phase five. PTG is an iterative process, one that, ideally, you do throughout your life.

LEARNING TO LIVE WELL

We want to leave you with two important messages before we move ahead. The first is that the conventional ways of dealing with trauma often leave people feeling stuck, damaged, and as though they have been sentenced to life as a diminished version of themselves. PTG offers another path: the opportunity to use trauma and struggle to create greater meaning, deeper purpose, and a life that is more authentic and fulfilling than you could ever have imagined. Either way, *you are still you*. When you walk the path from struggle to strength, the essence of who you are goes with you. You just get to leave behind all the secrecy, shame, guilt, and pain under which you've been hiding.

Remember that those who do well with this process are curious—about the world, about life, and about themselves. At his lowest point, Josh asked each of his friends to recommend books for him to read. This led him to read *Man's Search for Meaning* by Viktor Frankl, a Holocaust survivor, and *The Power of Myth* by Joseph Campbell. He also sought out meetings with people who seemed to possess the kind of fulfillment he wanted, and asked them about their lives. In Frankl, Campbell, and others, Josh began to find his way through the darkness that engulfed him.

You, too, can find your way out of the darkness. This book is about more than struggling well; it's about *living well*. In the next chapter, we continue the journey by addressing the first two areas of PTG in greater depth, giving you a clear understanding of how to strengthen your relationships and develop greater personal strength.

CHAPTER TWO

STRUGGLE WELL, LIVE WELL

———

"Strength and growth come only through continuous effort and struggle."[7]

—NAPOLEON HILL

KEN'S STORY: DISCOVERING THE SINE WAVE

During the wars in Iraq and Afghanistan, my team spent a lot of time analyzing sophisticated radio-controlled bombs. The task required us to look at frequency spectrums of different types of firing devices, which meant we were constantly viewing sine waves—the up and down, wave-like patterns that revealed a bomb's electrical activity. At times, the waves looked regular and gradual, a perfect example of an evenly spaced sine wave. Other times, the frequencies produced sharp peaks and valleys. Depending on the identified frequencies, we adjusted our procedures.

Life is just like a sine wave. It doesn't matter who you are—you will face struggle. You celebrate births and mourn deaths; cheer at marriages and weep over divorces; you win new jobs, and lose employment in layoffs. These ups and downs happen as regularly as the up and down curves of sine waves. Sometimes you manage to handle those ups and downs with a steady hand and a sense of calmness, like an evenly spaced wave. This type of response to struggle limits the peaks and valleys, and keeps you in an optimal zone of clear decision-making.

But other times, your reactions to struggle may turn volatile. If you're not careful, these types of reactions can be as destructive to yourself and your loved ones as a triggered bomb: there's an explosion.

In this book, we teach you how to respond, rather than react. What's the difference? A reaction is a quick, unconscious process. For example, maybe you have a tough day and some retail therapy seems like a good way to make you feel better. You go out and buy a brand new car, which immediately makes you feel great. But when the first bill comes four weeks later, you sink into depression, because you realize you can't afford to make the car payments. As shame sets in, you fall even deeper. You start feeling desperate for something else that can launch you back up, and the volatile trend continues. Realistic?

A response, on the other hand, is a conscious decision—like taking a deep breath before you yell at the kids for crashing your car. A response gives you the time to ask: what can I do to make this a learning point?

Responding to struggle enables you to keep the sine wave of life gradual and even, like rolling hills—navigable terrain. We call this the Response Sine Wave. Reacting to struggle, on the other hand, launches you above and then plunges you below the healthy middle zone, creating what we call the React Sine Wave. In the React Sine Wave, you're off-center and off-balance.

This chapter examines response strategies to keep you in the Response Sine Wave as you confront struggle. It also addresses the common ways you may end up in the React Sine Wave when trying to cope with struggle in unhealthy ways.

OPTIMAL LIVING: THE RESPONSE SINE WAVE

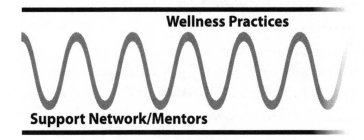

Let's think about those gradual rolling hills of the Response Sine Wave. Now, imagine you're in a car, driving on a well-paved road that takes you up and down those hills. A good driver takes into account the boundary of the shoulder, marked by a steady white line. On the other side, a solid yellow line indicates where your lane ends, and the oncoming lane begins. These boundaries are necessary; they provide the space for you to keep your car both from plummeting off the shoulder and from running into oncoming traffic. Similarly, our mode of living is healthiest when it functions within boundaries. Your car may weave a little bit, but at the end of the day, you need to stay between the lines.

Those lane boundaries contain the space that we call optimal living. When you're living optimally, you're able to maximize your natural capacity for balance, wellness, and your ability to heal. You can make conscious and active choices about the way you want to be. Rather than veering off the road at the first sign of trouble, you're able to steady your hands on the wheel and make a conscious decision about what you need to do with the car. Or, in this case: your life.

It's important to note that, ideally, those boundaries are formed before a crisis occurs. Imagine the construction crew painting those lines on our metaphorical road. They'll be much more effective and have an easier time if they paint when the weather's clear. Although it's possible for a crew to work during a thunderstorm, conditions are compromised all around. And although you might be able to muster the energy to build these boundaries during the midst of a struggle, you'll have a much easier time if you work ahead of the storms.

CHARACTERISTICS OF OPTIMAL LIVING

What does it look like when you're experiencing life in the Response Sine Wave? It's optimal living—a flourishing of all the domains of Posttraumatic Growth, discussed in Chapter One. Optimal living equips you to do more than merely survive times of struggle; optimal living sets you up to thrive in all areas of life. You're able to build a profound sense of your own strength. You have strong self-confidence, knowing that you can deal with any situation that may come, and respond to it in a way that's true to who you are.

This thriving comes inwardly and also outwardly. You develop the capacity to build deep and meaningful relationships with others. As you receive support and empathy, you grow in being supportive and empathetic. You are grateful for each day, each blessing, and each person that comes into your life.

When in the Response Sine Wave, you're able to view a

challenge as a growth opportunity, rather than bad luck or some sort of cosmic punishment—the proverbial black cloud. Living daily with this mindset helps you appreciate all of the possibilities that life presents you with. When one opportunity is foreclosed in your life, you immediately recognize that it's opening up other doors. Your stamina doesn't falter; it persists. Instead of thinking about giving up, you know that you're capable of doing anything. You can't be deterred.

So how do you ensure you remain in the Response Sine Wave, the place of optimal living? First, you need to create those boundary lanes.

SUPPORT NETWORK AND WELLNESS PRACTICES

Let's define these boundaries in practical terms.

On one side, you need a support network of quality people in your life who help keep you grounded. Although some people have large support networks, most people end up spending the majority of their time with three to five people—and that's plenty. If you can build a network of three to five people that care about you, listen well, and help lead you in a healthy direction, you've got a critical piece in place to help you live in that Response Sine Wave.

One person might be a close family member; another might be a supervisor at work. Another safe ear might be the friend you go to the gym with every day, or a counselor, or a mentor. What's most important is that you find people who listen well, show you they care enough to really understand how you're doing, hold you accountable, ask you hard contemplative questions, and don't judge.

Why? Because you become the average of the three to five people you spend the most time with. For that reason, it's critical to find people who have attributes that you admire and that you want in your own life—perhaps their principles, ways of living, a sense of kindness, integrity, or generosity. Through conversation, mentorship, and friendship, you'll learn what makes these people tick. You'll notice how they've become better versions of themselves through their own struggle.

On the other side of the Response Sine Wave, you need the boundary of wellness practices. Wellness practices are necessary to regulate your thoughts, feelings, and actions. They enable you to self-regulate, and if there's one thing we know for sure, it is this: if you cannot self-regulate, you self-medicate.

Practices such as meditation, exercise, reading, and deep breathing are all examples of activities that help you regulate your emotions when struggle hits. Some people pray; some people journal. Others do yoga, or hike, or archery, or kayak; others might read, enjoy music, or volunteer doing meaningful work. Different practices work for different people, but essentially, the practices that work best for you are centering; they'll enable you to find your sense of presence and balance. They lead to a sense of wellness that is critical for navigating times of struggle.

Often, wellness practices can lead you to a stronger support network. When you start exploring different ways of pursuing mental, physical, financial, or spiritual wellness, there are sure to be others in those environments that can become valuable to you. Stepping into a gym, a yoga class, or archery lane can bring you into contact with other people pursuing healthy living. If you're struggling with alcohol or another addiction, go to a twelve-step meeting. Even if you don't want to stop drinking entirely, you'll encounter people in that room who are trying to become better versions of themselves—and those might be people you need to get to know.

There's one other key factor that helps you remain within the marked lane of the Response Sine Wave—one as important as keeping your car in *drive*. If you want to respond to struggle in a healthy way, it's crucial to accept the fact that life brings you ups and downs. Struggle doesn't discriminate. If you can recognize that struggle is inevitable, no longer are you surprised when something bad happens. Instead, you can say, "Okay. This is life. Now I have to figure out what to do with it."

You don't personalize it; you work through it.

This notion of staying within the lane is meant to illustrate a sense of balance—what so many of us are trying to achieve in life. If you have a strong core, life might still knock you sideways, but you quickly regain your balance. These strategies offer a way to navigate back to the middle after temporarily being thrown off course.

STRONG WELLNESS TRIANGLE

There are concrete steps you can take in order to ensure that "balance" isn't just an abstract ideal, but that it becomes your reality. We've created the Wellness Triangle to help you create a fully balanced life. The outside of the triangle is made up of the three areas that need to remain healthy for optimal living: physical, mental, and financial. In the center of the triangle, we portray your spiritual wellness, represented within a sphere. This sphere could essentially be viewed as a balance ball: ideally, it touches all three sides of the outer triangle, ultimately holding it up.

The inside of the triangle illustrates the spirit, our soul—the "*why*" that should drive each of the outer areas. We believe this *why* is crucial. Although the triangle is one of the strongest geometric shapes known, without a strong center, the structure ultimately collapses. If that central area is weak, then you've got a hollow shell—one that won't hold up against the weight of hard struggle.

When any one of those areas is unhealthy, stress accumulates and your ability to maintain balance is thrown off. The resulting imbalance can end up jeopardizing your most valued areas of life. Let's consider a man with robust spiritual wellness: he wants to help save the world by starting a nonprofit. However, this person shows weakness in the financial wellness area, because he doesn't want to pay himself. This big-hearted person may end up so financially impaired he can't pursue his mission. Or consider a woman who works all the time. She has great financial wellness and loves her job, but doesn't take care of herself. Ultimately, she ends up sick because she's not eating right or exercising. She has to take a leave of absence from work, and ends up losing what she cares about most.

Balance, therefore, is crucial. In order to maintain a purpose-oriented life that makes the most of your passions and abilities, each of these four wellness areas must be maintained. Each area of the Strong Wellness Triangle is evaluated numerically from one to five, with a five denoting the best score, and a one describing the lowest score.

Life remains model

Let's go over each in more detail.

THE OUTER TRIANGLE: MENTAL, PHYSICAL, AND FINANCIAL WELLNESS

The outside of the triangle concerns areas that are easily observed by others; in that way, it can be viewed as your ego. And a healthy, balanced ego is a good thing.

When you're strong in the mental wellness category, you can **concentrate** on the task at hand with ease, are able to tap your **creativity** for problem-solving and enjoyment, and are passionately **curious** about yourself and the world around you. You can remember new information, and can learn new concepts and skills. You'll typically engage in practices that drive your mind to thrive, and you cultivate habits that spark curiosity and provide motivation.

Reading is one example of a mental wellness practice, an important habit of people trying to struggle well. Readers encounter inspiring authors who point them toward other inspirational works; by encountering new ideas and thought-provoking voices, readers are bound to grow in mental wellness. In our work with veterans, we also encourage meditation of different kinds. Other practices, such as breathing, walking, and yoga, can be helpful for mental wellness because they require clear focus in the present moment. It might be obvious that some mental wellness practices, like those we just mentioned, spill over into physical wellness practices as well.

Physical wellness is determined by **fitness, nutrition, and sleep.** When you have strong physical wellness, you are strong and flexible; you are fit enough to do what you want to do, eat well, and avoid unhealthy habits. After sleeping, you wake up feeling well rested.

Financial wellness is also key, because financial stress can negatively impact every other area of your life. Financial wellness is about your external environment; it can be evaluated based on **where you live, how you live, and how much you have to live on over the short, medium, and long term.** Building up financial wellness means having savings that allow you to weather storms; it means having a plan, having a budget, having a sense of predictability. Through using budgeting tools, consulting people who are financially successful, and being smart, you can generally avoid the overwhelming problems that financial stress can create. Bottom line—don't spend more than you make, and save for the rainy days!

THE INNER TRIANGLE: SPIRITUAL WELLNESS

We define spiritual wellness as the quality of your **relationships,** the amount of **service** you perform to yourself and others, and your strength of **character.** People experience a great deal of inner strength and peace by maintaining strong relationships. Those might be with family members or friends, they might exist within your community, or with a higher power. Each individual has different relationships that matter most.

We also believe a sense of service to others is key to maintaining the health of your spirit; it's important to live for something outside of yourself. Although our definition of spiritual wellness is not religious in nature, we still recognize our spiritual wellness values in many of the world's major religions. Jesus, for example, stressed the importance of loving your neighbor. It's no accident that Christians and non-Christians alike have returned to this value throughout history; those who have tried to love their neighbor usually experience a sense of fulfillment in serving others.

Even if the three areas on the outside of the triangle are in great shape, you'll have nothing more than an appealing exterior mask if there's nothing in the middle (Josh's story later in this chapter is a testament to this fact). With no "*Why*" directing your efforts, you build your life based on how the outside world perceives you. What leads you when there's no inner wellness? It's not a strong inner sense of conviction or character, or any direction coming from your personal values and beliefs—instead, it's fear of other people's judgment.

A strong spiritual core leads to a vibrant sense of feeling alive. There is purpose directing all of your efforts. Even though building up strong spiritual wellness often requires you to delve into "the abyss"—those unexplored places within you that may contain pain or shame—it is through strengthening spiritual wellness that your day-to-day experiences are most radically and positively transformed.

As we discuss spiritual wellness with people, we ask: How is the quality of your closest relationships? To what extent do you try to serve other people? How do you seek to make an impact on the world in a positive way? If your relationships are unhealthy and you only think about yourself, that ball in the center of the triangle starts to deflate. Without that central support, the triangle starts to collapse.

These practices are all built to lead you to a life of thriving. But perhaps it's easier said than done? If you are haunted by trauma, or reeling in the midst of struggle, this advice may seem hollow.

So let's put a face to what we're talking about.

KEN'S STORY: SEEKING TO THRIVE IN THE MIDST OF GRIEF

My dad and I were incredibly close, which I'm sure had a lot to do with losing my mom as a young boy. Although I spent over twenty-one years away from home in the Navy, my dad and I were best friends. We talked on the phone at least once every day. Even when I was stationed overseas, he and my stepmom got on a plane and came to spend time with my family.

When he died a couple of years ago, I was in a funk for about three months. I was still functioning and going to work every day. I was doing what needed to be done. We were building the retreat, which preoccupied me with something—in the standard prescription for grieving, staying busy is important. Still, there was a lot of grief.

But, because of the positive areas I had set up in my life, I was able to stay more in a "response" frame of mind. I had a great network of people and had my stepmom to care for. I had a lot to do to keep me grounded, which enabled me to carve out space to create a response.

I do my best to share some of the wisdom and knowledge that my dad shared with me; that's a way I'm able to continue keeping my father's legacy alive. For instance, my dad had these one-liners that I never forget. He used to say, "The two things a man must get right in life are his job and his mattress." He felt that most men spend the majority of their waking days at work, and to experience any element of wellness, you need to sleep. He'd say, "Do the math. The shortest period in any day is normally spent with the ones we love the most—and that's the time we screw up the most." He also used to say, "You only really leave two things behind on the earth when you die: your reputation and your children." Sharing bits like this is a way to prolong his impact and continue to build his and my positive reputation—the first component he knew he would leave behind. He also knew that his children would help form his legacy. Doing everything I can to struggle well in the aftermath of his death is a crucial way to honor the second component. It was important to him that both of those things be in a good place.

toxic

THRIVING, NOT MERELY SURVIVING

Ken's story may not provide the flashy picture you might envision when you hear the word "thriving"—the reality is that it was more of a daily choice to put one foot in front of the other, lean into his network of support, and choose to invest his time in meaningful ways. His funk could have lasted three years, rather than three months, and that's our point with this sine wave concept: we try to help people minimize the peaks and valleys, and then shrink the gap in-between them. We believe it's the daily choices that enable a person to respond in a healthy way, rather than reacting in a knee-jerk, volatile manner. If a person can pull that off in the midst of trauma, we call that thriving, indeed.

Taylor Morris, the young man whose story was shared in our Introduction, offers up another example of how a support network and wellness practices help a person thrive within turmoil. Losing both arms and both legs could have sent anyone into a deep depression, let alone a young man in the prime of his life. But in Taylor's case, his family and friends immediately mobilized around him: his support network was gathered. We put an iPad in front of him, which enabled him to have direct contact with friends still fighting in Afghanistan. Taylor knew his friends were worried about him, so he started reaching out to those friends, encouraging them while going through his own healing process.

Taylor's community helped him stay grounded and regain his inner sense of balance. Ultimately, through their support and his own efforts to reach out, he regained wellness and was able to start the emotional and physical healing process.

But what happens to people when they have to go through something tragic entirely on their own? What happens when there's no purposeful activity or wellness practices to keep them grounded? Without those boundaries in place, tragedy can easily cause you to career out of the lane. After you've landed in a ditch, it's going to be much harder to get yourself out than if you'd stayed close to a boundary line, pulled over, and taken a deep breath. That's why we advocate building up these elements of optimal living *before* the crisis hits.

Stories like Ken's and Taylor's serve as a reminder that struggle hits all of us—even the wellness expert, even the young and strong. These stories also remind us that each new struggle presents new challenges, forcing us to grow in new ways. But that's a good thing. We're always a work in progress. Every single day, in every chapter of our lives, we discover how to live better, and struggle better—to struggle well.

THE CHALLENGE TO LIVING OPTIMALLY

The Response Sine Wave describes balanced living; you're

driving right down the middle of your lane. Ideally, when struggle hits, you want to remain in that middle zone. You look in the mirror and steady yourself: "Yes, this is happening. It hurts, but I know what to do. I have people in my life I can reach out to. I have ways to clear my head. I can't change it, but I can be strong and respond to it."

But if it was easy or reflexive to do that, then we wouldn't be writing this book.

Let's be honest: life *is* struggle. Every day you wake up, open the door, and life slaps you in the face. Maybe you spill your coffee. Maybe you're stuck in traffic. Maybe you get into an accident, or you get bad news. Maybe you get an email informing you that your mistake just lost you your biggest client. You get an alert that your bank account was hacked, or you get a text from your significant other: "We need to talk." And that's just the minor stuff. Sexual assault, violence, war, abuse, natural disasters—those are all part of our reality too.

Something happens almost every day that tests you and throws you on defense. These daily slaps make this world of optimal living difficult, if not impossible. If there is no balance, wellness, or healing, the result is that you struggle poorly and you live poorly. You're thrown out of the Response Sine Wave and find yourself in danger-ous territory.

SYMPTOMS OF LIVING IN THE REACT SINE WAVE

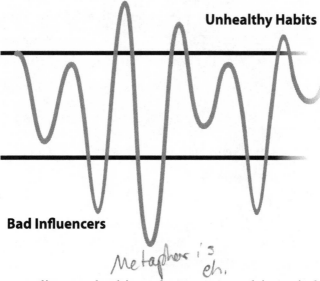

Unhealthy Habits

Bad Influencers

Metaphor's eh.

Struggling poorly ultimately gets you stuck in a mindset of reaction, putting you on that volatile roller coaster of the React Sine Wave. When good things happen, you're happy. When bad things happen, you're sad, or frustrated, or irritated. If too many bad things happen in rapid succession, you end up either constantly worrying about what's going to happen next, or agonizing over what already occurred. Life feels like a series of massive pendulum swings.

When life batters you with challenge after challenge, it can feel like there's no space to make any kind of conscious choice about how you want to be. You do the best you possibly can with the tools that you have, but essentially, you're constantly in react mode.

When you're *reacting* to struggle, you often behave or think in ways that are characteristic of PTSD symptoms. That doesn't mean that anyone experiencing life in some of the following ways should be classified as having PTSD; it simply means that trauma can cause similar reactions in people, across a spectrum. By identifying these common reactions, we can develop a plan to guard against them.

Above the Middle Zone: Fear and Anger

Above the thriving middle zone of the Response Sine Wave, the React Sine Wave might ratchet up into the zone of fear, termed "anxiety" by the mental health community. When you're operating from a place of anxiety or fear, you're not able to deal effectively with your present circumstances. Instead, your head remains stuck in the future and you focus mainly on the "what-ifs?" of what might happen next.

Soldiers learn to cultivate this "what if?" mentality on the battlefield, because it produces high energy, hyper-vigilance, and high-alertness. But if you don't turn down the hyper-vigilance that you needed in the streets of Baghdad, it makes for a very anxious life. You constantly worry about possible threats, which may or may not ever happen.

Because the stakes seem so high, you have little tolerance for mistakes—both from other people and from yourself.

You have enormously high expectations of yourself and others, again motivated by fear; if someone doesn't do something they should, *something bad could happen.*

When the hyper-vigilance and high expectations become overwhelming, you push the turbo button, pushing you even higher above the middle zone into either anger or rage. Rage seems to take the place of all other emotions, including fear. Although it often pushes you to a point of losing control, that explosion can still be a relief—you achieve a release for all the pent-up stress you've been shoving down. Unfortunately, it often results in more struggle immediately afterwards.

Rage functions like a volcano, one that erupts at random times with little apparent warning. The eruption of rage or anger may far exceed what's appropriate at a given time. After walking around for days with stress, fear, and anger building up slowly, all it might take is for someone to say the wrong thing—and then the volcano erupts.

Reacting above the middle zone leads you to frequently second-guess yourself, worrying that what you're doing is not good enough, not smart enough, not appropriate enough. This can throw off your ability to objectively consider even the most typical of conversations. Instead, you relive that conversation and question yourself. You're prevented from living in the present moment, because you're constantly kicking yourself about what you did and said, worrying you might do it again.

This anxiety can severely limit your life. If you've been robbed at an ATM taking money out, you may feel severe anxiety about ever returning to an ATM again. You'll always try to go inside the bank. Because of this anxiousness, you've now limited your options about how to go about basic life activities, like getting cash. That reflects a life out of balance—you're outside the healthy middle zone of optimal living.

Returning to that middle zone is going to require managing your anxiety and getting back to a point of self-regulation. When you walk up to that ATM, you'll be alert and vigilant, but not necessarily hyper-vigilant. You'll look behind you before you put your card in, and again before you take the money out. As you turn around, you'll make sure you can walk back into a safe environment. If you can manage your anxiety and bring it down to a more balanced level, your experience getting robbed might make you extra cautious, but it shouldn't limit your options in daily life.

Below the Middle Zone: Sadness and Numbness

Alternately, the React Sine Wave might plummet below the healthy middle zone into an area of sadness, called "depression" by the mental health community. When functioning in this mode, it's easy to become preoccupied with the past; you fixate over what you did or didn't do, or what happened. Remaining stuck in the past can leave you feeling deflated, disconnected, and unmotivated. You might struggle to muster the energy or desire to do anything. Maybe you don't think anything you do might make a difference; maybe you're simply jaded by past events and can't get beyond them.

Once again, this prevents you from dealing effectively with your present circumstances. To return to the driving metaphor, living with a backward focus is like trying to navigate your way toward your destination while only focusing on what's in the rearview mirror. That's no way to move forward.

Another symptom of the React Sine Wave is numbness, where you simply disconnect and shut down. You withdraw from life and other people and become unmotivated and disengaged. It's hard to get off the couch. Everything seems like too much effort to try to accomplish. Some people describe this as depression or simply profound sadness. It feels as though there's a black cloud hanging over you, and getting through your day feels draining and often pointless.

Disconnected Head and Heart

When living above or below the healthy middle zone—

when leaning into either fear or sadness—you fall out of balance. You're not present, you're not engaged, and you're not connected. We often describe this imbalance as being a symptom of a disconnected head and heart. When carrying intense sadness or anxiety, many people simply turn off their emotions entirely and become numb.

In part, that's done out of self-preservation. There's simply too much emotional weight from everything taking place—from the smallest item, like spilling coffee on yourself before you have to go into a meeting, to the bigger hits, like a major conflict with your spouse. If you were to take those daily struggles, internalize them, and feel them in your heart, it would be overwhelming. It would stop you in your tracks. Forget about functioning in react-mode; you wouldn't function at all.

We see this often in the veterans we work with. Men and women who have gone into combat have essentially learned to turn off their hearts. This has been a professional necessity. When you are dealing with death and destruction, losing friends and taking out enemies, you can't be empathetic. You've got to shut your emotions off to go do your job—but when you come home, you're eventually going to need to turn all that back on.

It's not just combat veterans who disconnect their hearts

and try to make it through their days without feeling. Imagine a child who encounters neglect at an early age. During those young, formative years, that child's heart is repeatedly broken and learns to shut off. As these children grow into adults, they try to live a normal existence, but exposing their emotions feels dangerous. Countless triggers serve as messages that they're not worthy, or not useful; adults like these may even get into relationships that repeat patterns of neglect. Empathy feels useless; survival is everything. These people may grow used to operating solely out of their heads, without listening to their hearts—they shut down the part of themselves that feels, dreams, and hopes.

Many Soldiers struggling with PTSD, or even patients in a psychiatrist's office, want to literally remove the parts of the brain that contain the pain. We've seen young vets getting their brains shocked in an effort to erase the agony. In World War I, they gave lobotomies to Soldiers with PTSD. They thought if they cut part of the brain out, the Soldiers wouldn't have nightmares anymore; they wouldn't have any trauma-related issues at all.

Some psychiatrists take this same approach when, as their first step of treatment, they put their patients on high doses of drugs. But when the drugs wear off, what happens? Should the patient expect to take those drugs for the rest of his or her life?

perpetuating stigma

Fucked up

It doesn't work to try to shock or medicate your brain to a place where the pain disappears. In essence, what those techniques are attempting to do is convince you that your thoughts aren't true, or that your memories aren't real. Trying to do that is like breaking off your rearview mirror so that you can convince yourself there's nothing behind you. But of course there is. It may even be necessary to look at it from time to time.

Our belief is that there's a way to get through this life, knowing that pain is in your rearview mirror, without having to constantly focus on it. How? You need to do the hard work of re-engaging your heart. The heart is the part of the system that injects new ideas, hope, positivity, feeling, and balance back into your system. It's the part that helps you determine your values, build up relationships, and maintain a focus on others.

We speak about the idea of balance a great deal in this book, because ultimately that is the place that makes thriving possible. While surviving solely from your head creates considerable pain and suffering, it is equally true that living only from your heart is also not such a good idea. When you're living solely from your heart, it's possible that you're so vulnerable, so sensitive, so open, that you're exposed. Living in a way that's purely guided by emotion takes away the self-regulation that is so crucial to keeping you within your boundary lanes.

The mental health and the nonprofit communities offer up some examples of how this can work out badly—something we've seen firsthand, working with nonprofits at our retreat centers. Some small nonprofits run their organizations with their heart, meaning that they've found a niche related to their passion—perhaps they're working with dogs that need to be adopted. If those nonprofits don't rigorously apply all the brain-related methods of healthy business operations, their passion ends up going nowhere. Maybe they don't realize how much money they need to pull off their business plan, or they don't know how to raise the funds. In many practical ways, it's not wise to rely solely on your heart.

Ultimately, what you want is a fusion between head and heart. That's where your power lies, where you're able to become your best self. It's where your spirit can thrive and flourish. This balance is a crucial part of living optimally—it's getting back to the middle of the sine wave. By using your head and your heart, you're able to unlock your full potential as an empathetic, kind, principled, and strong human being.

Don't forget about your internal cash register

When you're living without this balance, primarily above or below the middle zone in the React Sine Wave, you're just surviving. Your life is composed of a series of reactions, instead of responses. In other words, life owns you. However, if you can maintain your position in that middle zone of optimal living, it's you who owns life. By remaining grounded in a response frame of mind, you can avoid getting thrown out of the lane; you can even discover how to wring out every ounce of value from a bad situation.

Before we move back over to the sunny side though, we need to acknowledge some of the ugly ways that life in the React Sine Wave gets you in trouble.

UNHEALTHY HABITS

People rarely fall neatly above or below that middle zone. Frequently, you're some mix of both. Imagine yourself back in that car, sidelined on the shoulder. Now imagine that you try to get yourself out of your bad situation by essentially pressing the brake and the gas at the same time. What happens? You get stuck or spin in circles and can't seem to make progress. Ultimately, the brakes are going to heat up and burn out, or you're going to run out of gas.

The real-life version of this is just as bad for progress as the car analogy. We press the gas when we're living on edge, and we stomp on the break when we go numb and disconnect. The result? Exhaustion. We can't seem to get on top of anything. When we feel overwhelmed or stuck—when we feel numb or on edge—what we turn to aren't necessarily healthy cures. Usually, we're looking for something to provide comfort or some semblance of relief. If we're down, we want something to rev us up; if we're on edge, we want something to bring us down.

If you find yourself worn out by this volatile cycle, you might recognize a consistent problem: an inability to self-regulate. It's far more natural to *react* to your circumstances than take the time to *respond*, particularly if you haven't yet built up habits to force yourself back within the boundary lanes. As a result, the size of the swings becomes more dramatic, and the length of time you're stuck either above or below the lanes becomes more pronounced.

Addiction

We believe that those who cannot self-regulate will self-medicate. With no wellness practices for self-regulation, you may turn to things that are destructive and addictive, and come with a lot of side effects. The list of unhealthy coping mechanisms is long—drugs, alcohol, violence, hyper-sexual behavior, pornography, gambling. There's also over-spending, overeating, under-eating, over-working out, or under-working out. Maybe you're playing adrenaline games, bungee jumping, having an affair, or driving dangerously in the car—just trying to shake off the numbness and get some kind of spike.

The goal of self-medication is either to stop feeling

at all and usher in numbness, or it's an effort to feel *something*, through means of an unnatural high. Ultimately, what you're trying to do is find comfort. You're trying to find relief. You're trying to take some of the steam out.

What's clear though, is that self-medication doesn't give you real comfort. Maybe you get the temporary high you're looking for, but only briefly—and then you need a little bit more next time...and a little bit more next time. In addition, the self-medicating creates other destructive elements: it drains the bank account, alienates you from those you care the most about, or costs you your job. "Self-medication" turns out to be poison. It makes your already hard situation, far worse.

Bad Influencers

As we spoke about earlier, you are the average of the three to five people you spend the most time with. When you are struggling deeply, and your life is filled with unhealthy habits, it is easy to attract the wrong sorts of people, something demonstrated by the old cliché: misery loves company. These are the types of people who encourage you to come out on a Wednesday and drink until the wee hours of the morning, or to skip work. They might urge you to cheat on your spouse or partner, or blow off school, or give into your worst impulses.

These people are dead weight. They drag you down and prevent you from getting to a higher plane of living. Instead of helping you become the person you really want to be, they create a sense of complacency that, "Maybe, this is what it's *supposed* to be." You might start rationalizing your toxic behavior: "I'm just going to figure out the best way to cope. My choices aren't that bad—this is normal." You stop looking to rise above a destructive world, and instead give into it, destroying what you love in the process.

BROKEN WELLNESS TRIANGLE

Recall our earlier discussion of the Strong Wellness Triangle, and consider those categories in the midst of this destructive context. All four areas of wellness are likely compromised. If you're self-medicating, you're rapidly undermining your physical wellness. With no habits for self-regulation, your financial wellness is probably also falling apart. You've exchanged mental wellness for unnatural highs, which do nothing to heal your deep inner pain. And spiritual wellness? Forget about it.

Ultimately, your triangle breaks apart, and you become a mess. Mentally you can't concentrate; you feel trapped in a fog. You feel no sense of motivation. Essentially, you phone it in as best you can, but feel a total absence of curiosity or enthusiasm in doing so.

Physically, you're compromised. Maybe you *can't* do the things you want to be able to do—you try to walk up the stairs and feel out of breath. You can't sleep. Or perhaps you're simply abusing your body. Your body is supposed to be your temple; it's the vessel that enables you to do all other things. But in a place of self-destruction, you subject your body to abuse and neglect.

Financially, you have no savings. You've landed in a place of immense financial stress, and maybe you're making it worse by engaging in retail therapy, or gambling, or reckless spending to temporarily feel better. Fundamentally, you don't have the financial wherewithal to create any sense of comfort or confidence.

Most critically, your relationships are with people who

influence you toward self-destruction. These may be people who are not healthy, not trusting, not safe—or all of the above. More devastating still, you're really only concerned with serving yourself. There's no focus on the well-being of others.

JOSH'S STORY: A BROKEN WELLNESS TRIANGLE

Earlier I had spoken about the fact that my outer life had had no congruence with my internal life. I had shut myself off completely from listening to my heart, and my life—in no way—reflected what was true for me deep inside. These two triangles help illustrate that reality for me.

My outer triangle looked great. If we went back to 2011 and you met me, you would have thought my wellness areas were fives across the board. You would have seen someone smart, professionally successful, and well-educated. Mental wellness: five. You would have seen someone who physically was in great shape and looked good. Physical wellness: five. Financially, I looked like a five too. I had a beautiful house, beautiful cars, and all of the trappings of a life of material wealth. Financial wellness: five. You would have perceived that things were going really well.

But it was all a mask.

Underneath the surface, my real Wellness Triangle was

a complete mess. Mentally, my mind ran with constant thoughts of anxiety and fear. Panic attacks were a regular occurrence. I had a gnawing sense of not being good enough—this sense of constantly being just one mistake away from ruining everything. I regularly reviewed in my mind events that had taken place and anxiously anticipated the future.

Physically, I was hampered with crippling stomach pain that couldn't be explained by tens of thousands of dollars' worth of tests. Even more significantly, I was completely incapable of getting any sleep without the aid of pills or alcohol. Financially, my wife and I were in debt, despite making lots of money. We were spending every dollar we had, plus some.

Most crucially, the middle of my triangle—my spiritual wellness—was void. Deep and meaningful relationships with people, and acts of service for others were completely nonexistent in my life. Beyond valuing personal enrichment and a pursuit of some misguided definition of success, there was nothing there. What really drove me was how other people perceived me. When I started to really examine the life I had, I found something woefully inadequate. I was profoundly disconnected from anything true.

In many ways, I felt like I was living a *Truman Show* existence, where every part of my life was scripted by someone else. It was as if somebody else built my life and told me to live it. It felt foreign and disconnected from who I was and what I wanted—even if I didn't know yet what that was.

Unfortunately, I didn't yet have the framework of the Wellness Triangle to make sense of what was happening to me. I was surrendering the only life I'd ever known to pursue a life toward some sort of unknown. I had some inclination of where I wanted to be, but no idea how to get there. I thought perhaps some travel might do me good, and I explored the world for several months. It was fun but didn't get me any closer to where I wanted to go. I tried to shortcut again by trying to help other people, but that didn't work either.

After a long period of trying out methods that didn't help my inner emptiness, my one positive inclination to serve eventually led me to the veteran community. Thanks to Dusty's memorable call-out ("Unfuck yourself"), and the support of veterans I encountered, I began to do the hard work of building a new Wellness Triangle.

I decided I needed to find ways to break my old patterns and bad habits. I knew that if I continued to do the things I'd always done, I would get what I always got. Somehow, I had to catalyze learning situations for myself and get uncomfortable—a necessary step when you realize that you have no idea who the hell you are.

So, I tried different things to meet new people. I took up spin and met new friends. I went to twelve-step Al-Anon meetings. I asked my friends what books they read, and tried books I never would have considered before. I had lunch with people, told them my story, and got the opportunity to hear from them about their own times of struggle. For about a year and a half, I did the hard work of trying to reconstruct a Wellness Triangle and a life that was true to who *I* am, and filled in each area.

I had been a prisoner of my own mind and of my past training and experiences. Once I was able to escape that prison, life started to become joyous and fulfilling. That was only possible because I began to do the hard work of creating the life that I wanted and deserved. I did so by identifying and then living according to principles; finding trustworthy, principled, and high-integrity friends and mentors; and by cultivating practices that were sustainable and enduring. I didn't get there through my initial attempts to shortcut that journey.

I didn't find the freedom I sought until I took the long way.

PRACTICAL EVALUATION: YOUR WELLNESS CATEGORIES

Here's where the rubber meets the road. We've explained these ideas to you; now, it's your turn to begin applying them. Your healing and growth depend on your decision to do the work of examining your own life.

Ideally, the outside of that triangle supports your capacity to live out the inside of your triangle. A strong inner triangle—a sense of purpose, strong character, meaningful relationships, and service—needs to be supported by a strong outer triangle: solid mental, physical, and financial wellness. It's the strong combination of the inner and outer triangles that enables you to carry out your personal mission.

On a scale of one to five, rate your wellness on the blank Wellness Triangle provided.

The lowest score is one, and would be if:

- Your mind is completely scattered, and you have no interest in or ability to learn new things.
- Your body is inflexible, you are severely out of shape, and you never feel rested.
- Your finances are a complete mess and you are in significant debt.
- Your spirit is absent, and you lack any sense of character and purpose. Your relationships are weak, and you don't engage in any kind of service to others.

The highest score is five, and would be if:

- Your mind is focused, and you can learn new ideas with ease.
- Your body is in great shape, you can do anything you want, physically, and you sleep well.
- Your finances are in perfect condition with years of savings.
- Your spirit burns brightly, you have strong and healthy relationships, and you regularly serve others.

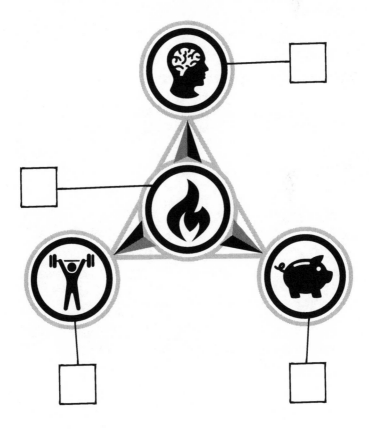

Be honest in your evaluation; it's important to have a clear starting place. Later in this book, we'll help you develop a series of goals to raise your lower scores. You'll develop an action plan to start targeting your most pressing problems. By the end of this book, you'll re-score this Wellness Triangle, and it's likely you'll have better numbers in each of those boxes.

By filling out the Wellness Triangle provided and thinking intentionally about where you're currently at, you've taken your first step into the abyss. Remember that there are scores between one and five: the numbers "two," "three," and "four" are all there to help you chronicle your progress. That's a good thing—a cave full of treasures awaits you!

CHAPTER THREE

LOOK BACK TO MOVE FORWARD

———

"Life can only be understood backwards; but it must be lived forwards."[8]

—SOREN KIERKEGAARD

It's not what's wrong; it's what happened.

Allow us to repeat that.

It's not what's wrong; *it's what happened.*

When dealing with trauma and times of deep struggle, the past plays a central role. You might fixate on the past, but without any particular purpose. The past obsesses you as you analyze what happened, who wronged you, and what you did to cause it.

grammar

On the other hand, you may try to ignore it altogether. The past is painful to think about, and why would you want to? Your focus is, instead, on simply moving forward.

Here's the catch: we know that understanding the past is essential to your ability *to* move forward. We've seen proof of that time and again in our work helping veterans achieve Posttraumatic Growth.

Let's return to the driving metaphor from the previous chapter. Imagine you've just started cruising down a scenic highway in your dream car. Now think about your rearview mirror. How often are you looking at it? If you're fixated on it, like some might be on the past, you can't drive the road ahead of you effectively. But if you never reference it at all, you run some serious risks. You might miss a car tailing you and get rear-ended; you might not notice the cop with his lights flashing; you might plow into another vehicle while changing lanes, and so on. Similarly, if you never acknowledge or examine your past at all, you seriously jeopardize your present.

That rearview mirror is helpful—it's there as a reference point to optimize your driving experience. We believe it's crucial to look back at your past constructively, so that you're able to figure out why you struggle with what you do, why you're good at what you do, and ultimately, so you can move forward, unhindered.

When you start to reflect on your struggle, it may become clear that it is often directly linked to the ways in which you were trained in your family of origin. It can be tempting to assume that these experiences define you—that they have come to form part of your core identity. But that's not true. You are not who you think you are; you are who you have been trained to be—in terms of your beliefs and your behaviors. If you want to be a different way, then you can be retrained. This is where understanding your past liberates you to move forward.

One of the key ways we make this process productive is by guiding you to look not simply at your bad experiences, but also the gifts you took away from your past. It's critical to honor your ancestors for the positive traits they instilled in you, whether it's a strong work ethic, a sense of humor, a love of music or art, a sense of service, or any other positive aspect of your upbringing. Everything in life is balance. You've got to be able to look at both the negatives and the positives in your past so that you can move forward with proper understanding.

We'll be even more specific about our goals. In guiding you through a reflection of your past, we want to accomplish three things. One: we want to stop any trauma you're dealing with from flowing to the next generation. Two: we want to show you the importance of disclosing your experiences in a safe setting, because disclosure is a major step toward kicking off Posttraumatic Growth. Three: we want to guide you to a fuller understanding of your past so that you can "retrain" yourself if necessary, and make a conscious decision about how you want to move forward.

THE CASE FOR ACE

War is one of the worst things humanity has to offer. In battle, Soldiers do their best to save the lives of their fellow warriors and their own while getting shot at; at the same time, they're shooting other people and taking lives. There's a reason veterans are often viewed as being in their own category of mental health: war adds one more dimension of complexity onto trauma.

But we're not mental health experts. Neither of us have a counseling degree. So why would we be qualified to speak about effective mental health approaches in helping people achieve Posttraumatic Growth?

Our qualifications come from the fact that we've seen what works and what doesn't. We've worked with men and women who are deeply knowledgeable, on all sides of this issue. We've seen through our work the transformative success of what a program like ours does for somebody.

Really big name

When Boulder Crest Retreat Virginia first started hosting veterans, we didn't yet have a program of our own in place;

we simply wanted to make a space available to people who were interested in improving the lives of veterans and military families. As a result, we ended up hosting a number of nonprofit programs, all of which had the same general goal: to help veterans live well.

The problem was, few of them accomplished that in a meaningful way. As discussed in our Introduction, many of these programs were "catch-and-release" and didn't lead to long-term healing. In fact, the way veterans described most of these programs is that they would sit around the fire, sing "Kumbaya," and tell war stories.

What puzzled us was the fact that, for many of these veterans, the trauma didn't seem to be derived primarily from their war experience. Most people described their experience in war as mixed; it was "the best of times and the worst of times." If that was true, then their war experiences didn't explain the whole of their struggle.

Along with some of the less-effective programs, there were some thoughtful, interesting people who brought a different perspective to the table. They broadened their scope of what might be fueling struggle, and seemed to get much better results. One of those people is Suzi Landolphi, who got us interested in the role that Adverse Childhood Experiences (ACEs) play in people's journey from struggle to strength.

Why didn't they research treatment?

Suzi had been doing work with veterans in California and started to realize that Soldiers' trauma often had more to do with what happened *before* they joined the military, than what happened *during* their time of service, including war experiences. Suzi examined what drove someone into the military in the first place—and how those past experiences might continue to impact veterans after they stepped off the battlefield.

Initially, we had come to the table with no starting assumptions about why certain people struggled well and others didn't; we had no framework in hand. Because we had an open mind, we were open to the possibility that the source of trauma wasn't necessarily what people assumed—which, in these Soldiers' cases, was usually the war. Our curiosity made us listen, observe, read, and ask a lot of questions. And whatever Suzi was doing seemed to be working.

From the beginning, our goal was to understand what was required for combat veterans to live great lives; we wanted to help them achieve long-term wellness, not give them a short-term Band-Aid. If we wanted to truly impact the largest number of people, we needed to build a model where the program "graduates" could then help other people from a healthy place, not from the injured place they started.

Suzi's research-based approach seemed to produce the

kind of deep, long-term healing we wanted to achieve, so we brought her in to work with us. Starting with her model, we began working through a diagram that looked at the positives and negatives from a person's upbringing.

It immediately became apparent to everybody working with their family tree diagram, especially the people filling them out, that the experiences they had in childhood were directly linked to their current struggles. It didn't matter whether that current struggle related to issues of anxiety or depression, alcohol or drug abuse, domestic or sexual violence, relationship challenges, or any other issues—consistently, there was a direct correlation between the experiences they had in their upbringing, and what they were struggling with at the current moment.

We began to really dig in, exploring the notion of childhood development, childhood trauma, and ACEs. The essential question we were trying to answer was twofold: why is it that people struggle? And why is it that some people can use their struggle to create strength and growth, while other people can't?

WHAT WE DISCOVERED: THE IMPACT OF CHILDHOOD

The discoveries we made led us to suspect that all trauma is not created equal. Trauma seems to have a more lasting effect depending on when it occurred. In particular, ACEs were especially far-reaching in their future impact. Children are often powerless to change their circumstances, because they're reliant on their caretakers for food, clothing, and shelter. Children, especially between zero and five years old, are in the midst of massive development, specifically related to their brain, their socialization, and their relational connections. As a result, traumatic experiences that occur during childhood make a deeper and longer-lasting impact than experiences which happen later in life, when there's more opportunity to change a bad situation.

Essentially, we learned that childhood trauma reduces a person's ability to deal with times of struggle. Struggle tends to cause people to revert back to whatever they were exposed to as "normal" while growing up—and if "normal" included alcoholism, violence, sexual abuse, or some other detrimental behavior, then a person's reversion may include some of those same damaging habits. Understanding this shed some light on our questions; perhaps this was why some people seemed to grow through their struggles, while others seemed to remain beaten down.

Let's say we were working with two Soldiers who went to war and saw the same level of death and destruction on the battlefield. After returning home, Soldier 'A' plugs along and continues with life in a way that seems relatively healthy. But Soldier 'B' seems to fall further and further behind; perhaps she's self-medicating, not sleeping, having nightmares. Most often, we discovered, what causes the differential between the two is normally childhood trauma.

Bold claim. Evidence?

It also became clear to us that there's no such thing as "simple" trauma, the idea that trauma can be traced back to a single incident. It feels easy to pin all of our struggles on one hard experience—"It's the divorce, that's what caused everything." But that ignores our complexity as humans.

Consider the rucksack that Soldiers carry—it's a full pack, a heavy pack. Throughout life, you fill your rucksack up with experiences, both good and bad. Then a traumatic event hits that's massive: a huge rock is added, and the pack can no longer be carried. But the truth is, you were already carrying plenty in that pack before the addition of the giant rock. Those pre-existing experiences help contribute to the weight of the current situation. Depending on how heavy they are by themselves, they might prevent you from ever putting the pack back on. And then, you're stuck.

How do you get unstuck? You need to examine what's in the rucksack. Until and unless you understand the experiences you carry—the rocks in your bag—you will only ever manage to be the sum of your past training and experiences. By pursuing an understanding of your past, you can repack the bag. You can keep your gifts and utilize them, and eliminate some of the heavier baggage.

TRAINING AND RETRAINING

If you take a good, hard look at the parts of yourself that you wish to change, you'll likely find that the barriers to improvement are related to how you were trained as a child. Similarly, the areas where you excel also tie back to your training. Your childhood experiences, therefore, are predictors of your current struggle and behaviors.

If you want to be an entrepreneur, but you can't get past your own fear of failure, that fear of failure might be linked to childhood experiences which taught you failure wasn't acceptable. As an adult, that fear of doing the wrong thing might prevent you from taking necessary risks. This is why we believe it's so necessary to go back and understand the past. You need to understand what might be standing in the way of you achieving your goals and living up to your full potential.

Perhaps you had an alcoholic father; as an adult, you might find yourself on one side of an extreme spectrum. Either you struggle as an alcoholic yourself, or you've committed to avoiding alcohol entirely. Or maybe, like the two of us, you had parents who worked all the time. In adulthood, you might find yourself gifted with a similarly strong work ethic, but might also struggle to make time for your family.

We don't bring this up to merely point out a trick of forecasting. Here's where this gets really important: your struggles rarely impact just you. It's not just your own goals that may be impeded by your past struggles. As the saying goes, hurt people, hurt people. If you don't take the time to closely examine your own pain, you not only obstruct your own success, you are at risk of doing to others the painful things that were done to you.

Unfortunately, bad behaviors might emerge even if you recognize the trauma in your past and commit to avoiding it in the future. Without probing that trauma for deeper understanding, your attempts to stop the negative generational cycles may often remain incomplete at best, or at worst, damaging in a new form.

How so? Overcorrection can be as dangerous as no correction. If you grew up in a house with lots of verbal abuse, you may end up getting into relationships where you don't share your thoughts or feelings at all, because you're trying to avoid confrontation at all costs. It feels nearly impossible to find the balance that is required for healthy living and healthy relationships.

If this is true, then is there any hope for breaking generational cycles? Our answer to that question is a resounding "YES."

We believe that we are the sum of our training and experiences, until and unless we understand them. People say "I am the way I am." But that's not true. You are the way you were *trained* to be. There are deliberate steps you can take to retrain yourself in a way that enables you to move forward with a lighter rucksack.

Our belief in this concept is based on the fact that we have repeatedly seen people conquer their demons, once they build their awareness of where and how those demons originated. This is true even for struggles with the label "genetic predisposition," like alcoholism. People have come to us with alcoholism flagged all over their family trees, and yet we've seen those people develop the capacity to free themselves from struggle through gaining a fuller understanding of the past.

Humans have an enormous capacity to evolve, change, and grow; that concept is at the core of this book and our lives. We don't want to simply give you tips on how to get through difficult times; we want to train you to struggle well and live well.

What does this retraining look like? A big piece goes back to what we laid out in the previous chapter; if you're looking to make deep changes in your life, you need a strong three-to-five network of support around you, and you need good wellness practices to help you self-regulate. It's also crucial to build a deep understanding of the origins of your life's trauma and gifts. Finally, we believe disclosure of this understanding is a necessary component of moving forward, something we'll soon discuss in greater length.

Sharing + Connection

A NUANCED PERSPECTIVE OF THE PAST

"Well, my dad was an abusive alcoholic. That's why I'm so messed up."

It's tempting to blame people and experiences for your lingering baggage. Perhaps this may be warranted, but it's counterproductive to do this in a shortsighted way. The statement above expresses this tendency: you want to pin your struggles on someone or something, but without any nuance. People and experiences are lumped in categories of only bad, or only good. We think it's important to take a thoughtful and comprehensive look at your experiences so you can understand them.

In studying your past experiences the way a scientist might, you get some distance from them. This increased distance saps some of these painful experiences of their loaded emotion, enabling you to get to a place of reflection and objectivity.

We fundamentally believe that everything in life is about balance—that's what we're striving for. That's what the sine wave is about, and that's what the Wellness Triangle is about—balance. We're not trying to find lives that have no struggle in them. We're not trying to live in "highs" all the time. We're trying to find some balance, because balance enables us to stay grounded.

In order to achieve balance when examining your past, you've got to look at the good stuff *and* the bad stuff. Recognize what was difficult *and* what was positive. Nobody is all one or the other.

KEN'S STORY: FINDING THE GOOD

Probably the first trauma I saw, other than the death of my mom, was the abuse from my grandfather in Pittsburgh. Although he never hit me, he was abusive to my grandmother and fought with my uncle countless times. When I stayed with my grandparents, I usually slept on the couch in the living room—they raised four kids in a tiny house, and when my aunts and uncles were home, there was nowhere else for me to sleep. My drug-addicted uncle would come in late at night and encounter my grandfather, who was usually drunk. That would turn into a knockdown, roll-around fistfight, which would literally happen right in front of me.

I watched that stuff for maybe seven or eight summers.

When he was sober, my grandfather was a great guy. He didn't drink on Saturday or Sunday, which meant weekends were great. But on the weekdays, it was normally pretty bad, especially Friday nights—he'd go straight from work to his club. Eventually though, around the time I was fifteen, he quit drinking altogether.

My grandfather was always a grumpy old man, but in a lot of ways, he was great to be around. He was a career Army veteran from both WWII and the Korean War. I remember many wonderful things about him including long walks in the forest hunting mushrooms. There were a lot of hard times with my grandfather, but there are some great memories as well.

During those summer days, to get out of the house, I'd go spend time with my friends, or I'd swim hundreds of laps in my neighboring uncle's pool. I figured out ways to make money by doing paper routes or selling donuts. Those summers built up my community, my physical strength, and gave me my first experiences as an entrepreneur.

Granted, I was exposed to violence—and that might be connected in some ways to becoming "a problem child" as a teenager. But luckily, I found my way into hockey. That turned into a productive way to harness any lingering violence I might have had in me. My experience as a hockey player produced some of the best experiences in my life. I was made captain of my team, which helped me develop as a leader, and encountered a number of service opportunities later on, through coaching and playing on a Navy exhibition team in Scotland.

I can think of other tough memories that ended up being useful. My mom's battle with cancer and her eventual death were obviously traumatic. Because she had a rare form of liver cancer, she was in a hospital in Washington DC, about an hour away from where we lived at the time. My dad was trying to work and raise kids, and also spend time with his wife who was in the hospital. That was rough for all of us.

Years later, when I was playing hockey in Glasgow on this exhibition team, a lady approached us. "Every time you guys play hockey you get a full crowd," she said. "We've got this hospice program that we're trying to raise money for—we'd love it if you could figure out a way of helping us." That was the first time I'd ever heard of hospice, and I remember thinking, "How cool could that have been for my mom?" We ended up doing a fundraiser for the hospice program and raised around $5,000. That was one of my first major opportunities to raise money for a cause I truly cared about.

It goes the other way too—some people or experiences that you remember as mostly good have their own hidden pain. My dad was probably one of the kindest men you'd ever meet, and he was also a workaholic. We didn't see him a lot. As an adult, I've done the same thing to my kids, which I regret. Because I was in the military, my daughters didn't see me through much of the time they were growing up. In hindsight, I wish I'd been a more available father; one of my current goals is to be a more present grandfather than I was a dad.

COMPASSION AND UNDERSTANDING

Like Ken, if you take a good, hard look at some of your most formative experiences, you'll usually find both gifts and pain; both good and bad. In identifying those nuanced layers, you'll often find reasons to feel compassion for the people in your life that you most want to blame.

Take Ken's grandfather, for instance. Maybe he drank because of his childhood, or the two wars he fought in, or maybe his job caused a ton of stress and that's why he didn't need to drink on the weekends. It's almost certain he wasn't drinking just to cause pain to his family.

Almost no one sets out to deliberately hurt other people. No one looks in the mirror and says, "There's an asshole." For the most part, everyone's trying to do the best they can. It's an unfortunate human tendency that, when life gets overwhelming, people often take their stress out on the people they love.

If you superficially label anything as wholly bad, or wholly good, or wholly anyone's fault, then you're playing checkers in a world of chess. When you examine the complexity of each painful experience, and each participant in that experience, usually you're able to discover compassion and understanding. That empathy, in turn, is enormously freeing. If you're able to forgive the people in your life who caused you pain by building up empathy for them through understanding, then you are in a place to better forgive yourself for your own struggles.

It's easy to forget that the people who caused you pain might have been in pain themselves. When you're a kid and things happen to you that don't seem fair, you make it personal; that's the natural inclination children have. If you get abused or mistreated in some way, you assume it's because you deserved it. Children of divorced parents often conclude that they were at fault for their parents splitting up, and they must therefore be bad kids. As an adult, you can see that those conclusions are totally off-base—and yet, those same conclusions might be at the root of your own current struggle.

This can lead us to personalize struggle to an unhealthy extent, and may ultimately prevent us from making peace with the past. The struggling woman whose parents divorced when she was a kid may have gotten stuck on the idea that it was her fault; as a result, she feels unworthy of love, and struggles in her own relationships. Maybe she pins her worth entirely on her romantic partners and her struggles compound every time a relationship doesn't work out. She might place the blame for this entirely on her parents, even as she continues her own negative cycle.

The whole point is that it's not about you. People personalize things that they shouldn't personalize. Somebody's own struggle does manifest itself in the way they treat you, but that's not a statement on your character or your value. It's a statement on someone else's struggles.

Painful experiences in childhood can also leave you with the sense that you're not valuable, and this becomes a huge stumbling block as you try to navigate struggle as an adult. Neglectful parents who don't nurture and support a child, or fail to communicate that the child is loved or worthy, can leave a lasting impression on that child of no internal worth. Overly involved parents communicate the same message, if they convey to their children that their worth is tied to their accomplishments and successes, rather than a sense of innate value.

With no sense of internal worth, you attach your value to other things, such as people, status symbols, material goods, or even some type of employment, as in the case of the military. When you're a big, fit, strong Marine, you have a strong sense of who you are and that you're worth something. However, if any one of these sources of value is taken away, you're not just losing a thing, you're losing a major piece of your identity. When that big, fit strong Marine is discharged and is now without the source of his worth, he may seriously struggle.

JOSH'S STORY: BUILDING EMPATHY THROUGH UNDERSTANDING

One of the things that Suzi loves to stress when it comes to childhood trauma is that it isn't always the big, obvious traumas that create the hardest struggle. Suzi calls these other types of traumas "emotional paper-cuts," and they can add up quickly. I am her poster child for this type of experience because from the outside it would be difficult for someone to understand my struggle. However, when you dig under the surface, things begin to make more sense.

Throughout my childhood and adolescence, my actions were informed by two responsibilities—ones that weren't so much assigned, as assumed by Young Josh. One was to ensure that my mom was happy. The second was to achieve in ways that would capture my father's attention and make him proud to call me son. Trying to balance those two priorities left one major component out of the picture: any sense of what I wanted to do. The lens through which I viewed the world was dominated by, "What will my mother feel about this, and will my dad approve of it?" All of my actions were based on how I perceived things would play externally. That was important because the external validation was critical to filling the inner void that I felt. I derived all of my worth and value from the accomplishments that I could achieve and the people I could please.

I've talked about the fact that I had built a Wellness Triangle solely based on ego, and that I was only concerned with how others perceived me. That led to my massive personal crisis as an adult, and can be directly linked to my childhood training and experiences. Given what I've relayed in the previous paragraph, it would be easy to blame this all on my parents. But let me tell you some of the fuller picture of what was going on.

My dad grew up largely away from his parents. His parents worked eighteen hours a day, seven days a week. They didn't have time to raise him, so that was the role of hired help, and when he got older, he was sent to military school. The message he got was that he was not worthy of his parents' time, love, or attention. A parent's presence was not something he witnessed; his idea of a parent was somebody who was out working to provide for the family. As an adult, he took up this same pattern: he worked incredibly hard and was gone a lot.

My mom grew up bullied by her own mother. My grandmother viewed my mom as competition for her husband. There's even a family video—from my grandparents' fiftieth anniversary celebration!—depicting my mom walking hand in hand with her dad, and on the video recording you hear my grandmother say, "There goes Sharon again, stealing my husband." That bullying created severe challenges for my mom, including a lack of self-worth and difficulty building relationships with other women. The message she got growing up was that she was a negative presence in her family, and that she was worth less than nothing.

Are these accurate diagnoses?

In my dad's absence, my mom was left alone; as the baby of the family, I was usually the one left with her. I felt like my responsibility was to take care of my mother, so that when my father was around, he would be happy to be with me.

I wish that I'd developed a strong sense of inner worth earlier on, but my parents didn't have that to give me. How could they give me what they didn't have? My dad had me subconsciously repeating the same pattern that he engaged in as a child: impress with achievements. My interpretation of my mom was that I needed to care for her because she was in a vulnerable position. Their training and experiences became part of my inheritance, and part of my own struggle.

The codependent relationship I had with my mom and constant striving for external validation and self-worth were obviously not great. At the same time, I also inherited a ton of incredible gifts from my parents. They both had service-oriented careers they were passionate about—my mom was a teacher, and my father is a doctor; together, they communicated an insistence on living out your passion. They gifted me an incredibly strong work ethic. I got an amazing sense of adventure from my mom and a profound sense of discipline from my dad. I gained empathy and kindness from my mom, and a love of reading from my dad. My deep sense of curiosity about the world comes from both of them. Is that right?

Each of my grandparents also passed on beautiful gifts to me. My mom's mother—who can be judged harshly from the above story—was a concert pianist and a music therapist in a mental hospital. My love of music comes from her. My dad's mother taught me that you are never too old to change, and you must live fully until the very end. Both of my grandfathers taught me about the importance of being kind to strangers, and to honor the story that every human being has inside.

I've learned that what's arguably unhealthy on one side has tremendous value on the other. Some of the experiences I went through during my childhood led me to the hardest season of my life; other experiences from that same period of time have enabled me to live the amazing, fulfilling, and joy-filled life I'm living now. On the other side of a great deal of exploration, disclosure, and reflection, I value all of the experiences of my upbringing, and know that each helped me become the man I am today. That knowledge brought compassion, forgiveness, love, appreciation, and understanding not only for my family, but for myself.

LAUNCHED INTO THE REACT SINE WAVE: CHILDHOOD TRIGGERS

In considering the impact of childhood experiences, it's worth revisiting the concept of the React Sine Wave. As discussed in Chapter Two, the React Sine Wave illustrates what life looks like outside of the optimal living zone. Ideally, you want to stay in the balanced middle zone, the place where you're able to remain calm and collected in spite of life's daily punches. In the healthy middle zone, you're able to maintain a sense of connectedness between your thoughts, feelings, and actions—i.e., your head and heart—and you experience joy.

When you're living in the React Sine Wave territory, you're out of that healthy middle zone. Often, it's your negative childhood experiences that launch you either above the middle zone, into a place of fear, or below that middle zone, into a place of sadness. A life that would otherwise remain balanced, and a person who would otherwise remain secure, can be thrown completely off course by the triggering of an unprocessed childhood event.

Struggle can be generated and fed when ACEs are un-witnessed, unprocessed, and un-reflected upon. If you lived in an abusive household that thrived on fear, you're going to end up with a great deal of anxiety. If you lived in a house where there was neglect or serious dysfunction, you're going to end up living in a world of sadness. In our work with people—including those with and without PTSD—we most often see that they experience a mix of both anxiety and depression.

In many ways, emotions can be compared to colors. Consider the color wheel you may have learned about in middle school art class. The primary colors are red, blue, and yellow; from those colors you can create any number of other shades. Similarly, there are three primary emotions: joy, fear, and sadness. The same way those three primary colors can account for every other color, those three primary emotions, in different combinations, can create any emotion.

Anger results from the combination of fear and sadness— and it's one of the most commonly triggered emotions from past trauma. Take road rage, for instance. Traffic can inspire irrational anger because of the ways it might tie back to past experiences that drummed up fear and sadness. If you grew up in a house with alcoholics who constantly prevented you from being able to do the things you wanted to do, all of a sudden that's where your mind goes when you're stuck on the freeway. Maybe you had to miss a sleepover because your mom wasn't sober enough to drive you, or you weren't able to get to school on time because you had to give your younger siblings breakfast while your dad slept off a hangover. Being stuck in traffic can put you back in that place of feeling prevented from moving forward by forces you can't control. It's not that you get angry at traffic. What bothers you is constantly having your momentum stopped.

JOSH'S STORY: LATE AGAIN!

When I was a kid, my mom was late a lot—and sometimes hours late. I was late to various school plays and sporting events that I was involved in. Not only was this inconvenient and embarrassing, it made me believe I was unimportant to my mom. The message communicated by her lateness was that I wasn't worthy of remembering; I wasn't a priority.

For a long time, if I was supposed to get together with somebody and they were late—especially when they didn't communicate that—I would get enormously irritated. My anger would far outstrip the level of the offense, and smoke started to boil out of my ears.

That was driven by two things. Number one, I felt a deep sense of sadness about these experiences I had as a child, when I felt like the unwanted kid. Number two, it created the fear of painful moments repeating themselves. Often, the relatively mundane experiences that can create the largest impact when tapped into, are experiences that communicate the person is not valuable—as in my case. That message can easily be internalized from various childhood experiences, which often lead to negative behaviors.

I've made this conscious now, spoken with my mom about it, shared with the people around me, and created my own game plan for dealing with the inevitable—people are late at times. When it happens, I take a deep breath, call or text the person to check in, and then find something else to do. I wait like an adult. But that self-awareness has been necessary in getting myself past the rage, to a place of self-mastery.

Our past experiences can cloud our capacity to see how to respond in the situation. If there's been no effort to understand or process past events, then we set ourselves up to default into react mode. Our past throws us right outside of the balanced middle zone.

ACE: THE ORIGIN OF STRUGGLE

As we mentioned, the research that Suzi brought to the

table that we found to be so effective in our work with veterans, concerned a fast-growing collection of studies which examine the impact of Adverse Childhood Experiences. One of the main people responsible for pioneering these studies was a physician named Dr. Vincent Felitti.[9] In 1985, he ran an obesity clinic as part of a Preventative Medicine program with Kaiser Permanente. Although Felitti's program was highly regarded and known for its efficacy, he had a consistently high drop-out rate with his obesity clinic patients.

In an effort to understand why this particular clinic wasn't getting better traction, Dr. Felitti began doing background research and surveys with his obesity patients. He discovered that most of his patients did not gain weight gradually over time, but went from relatively healthy weights to obesity over a short span. This puzzled him, as did a response one patient made during a survey interview, after he accidentally misspoke when asking her a question. He meant to ask his patient, "How old were you when you were first sexually active?" Instead he asked, "How much did you weigh when you were first sexually active?"

The website "ACEs Too High" describes this interaction: "The patient, a woman, answered, 'Forty pounds.' [Dr. Felitti] didn't understand what he was hearing. He misspoke the question again. She gave the same answer, burst into tears and added, 'It was when I was four years old, with my father.'"

In this woman's case, the experience of being sexually abused created a direct link to her obesity; another patient with a similar past describes why this may have been. "Overweight is overlooked, and that's what I needed to be." Dr. Felitti expanded his research questions to more consistently ask patients about a history of sexual abuse and was floored to find that the majority of his patients had similar trauma in their pasts. They had turned to weight gain as an emotional comfort, and because it felt like a source of protection.

Over the years, Dr. Felitti has been joined by countless other researchers who are examining the connection between childhood trauma and adult psychological struggles, such as addiction, PTSD, anxiety rates, and other issues. The body of research on ACEs has upended what the scientific community thought they knew about many of these issues, and is providing new frameworks to help patients achieve lasting wellness.

Several of these studies piqued our interest in particular—such as the one described in the article, "Childhood Traumas More Common in Military Members."[10] We learned that children who grew up in unstable environments, and who were exposed to a large number of

Adverse Childhood Experiences, often found their way into the military because it offered stability and a positive network of support. While acknowledging that most people who join the military "do so for reasons of altruism, patriotism, and self-improvement," the authors of the study also noted that, for some, the military offered an "escape from troubles." This was eye-opening for us. If a person had signed up for the military for its system of support, experienced challenges or trauma while serving, and then lost that system of support when they were discharged—wouldn't that person struggle even more as a civilian?

The article, "Trauma Before Enlistment Linked to High Suicide Rates Among Military Personnel, Veterans," also deepened our understanding.[11] Essentially, this article reported that people who go into the armed forces with a host of ACEs already in their background are more likely to struggle with suicidal thoughts after the stress of combat. Why? "A child experiencing abuse has little opportunity to effectively cope when stressed, being in a powerless position with no recourse. This may lead to less ability to handle future stressful circumstances." And— according to the previous study we mentioned—that's a much higher percentage of the military population than the civilian population.

So here's a common story: a Soldier signs up for the military as a way to escape a traumatic home life, then has multiple deployments and battle stress piled on top of this original trauma, and comes home struggling with PTSD. Although it's common to blame a veteran's PTSD on their experiences in war, this research suggests that's only the tip of the iceberg. For deep healing, it's necessary to go back further, and start where the trauma first originated. We saw this anecdotally in watching the effectiveness of Suzi's approach, compared to other efforts to help veterans, and have now seen it abundantly substantiated in scientific research.

What counts as an Adverse Childhood Experience then? The research breaks it down into three categories: the first, abuse, which may occur physically, emotionally, and/or sexually. The second category describes neglect, in both the physical or emotional realms. The third category of ACE is household dysfunction, which can include mental illness, a mother treated violently, divorce, an incarcerated relative, and/or substance abuse. Depending on your "ACE score," you may be more or less likely to struggle developmentally, behaviorally, or socially. Essentially, when ACE scores are high in a given individual, that person's resiliency and positive health are threatened.[12]

Perhaps you're reading the list above with a sinking feeling—recognizing that you have a number of those experiences in your own past. Are you doomed to struggle with PTSD as an adult? Will you be forever sidelined in dysfunction?

What about those who have a high score but are resilient

Not hardly. We share this information to emphasize just how crucial it is to take up the practices we endorse in this book. We have helped thousands of struggling people heal and grow, after experiencing serious trauma as both children and adults. Because of the healing and growth we've witnessed in our program, we believe that much more strongly in the efficacy of the methods described here, such as the boundaries described in Chapter Two.

If you can establish a strong Wellness Triangle and Response Sine Wave boundaries by having wellness practices, and creating a strong support network around you, then new adult traumas shouldn't take you off track. Yes, they may still cause short spikes in the sine wave; life might still launch you into a rollercoaster. But just because you had a tough childhood doesn't guarantee the rollercoaster is going to come off the tracks. Perhaps these past experiences have created patterns in your life that are easy to default into—but there are steps you can take to retrain yourself. You can create a new path for yourself.

Recently, we met with a former Soldier who had around eight ACEs in his background, but he has achieved great quality of life. The military enabled him to be productive and rise beyond his past. In fact, statistics show that military service for a male is the only break in the correlation between high ACE scores and low quality of life; in every other instance, a high ACE score usually means a person experiences a low quality of life.[13] Why? The military equips people with some of these healthy boundaries we just identified. This explains why it is so critical to translate some of the elements of what makes military training so successful into the civilian community, and was a critical driver of us deciding to write this book.

But it's not just these two boundaries that heal the damage left by your tough childhood experiences. One of the ways we define a "warrior" is somebody who's not a product of their environment or a victim of circumstance. It's someone with the capacity to rise above their upbringing. The only way you do that is by understanding it. You need to take a look in the rearview mirror. *Meditation*

LOOKING BACK TO MOVE FORWARD

"Until you make the unconscious conscious, it will direct your life and you will call it fate."[14]

—CARL JUNG

Problems you aren't aware of or don't acknowledge have a power over you that you can't see. And if you can't see it, you can't change it. Rather than being in control of your life, life is in control of you.

[handwritten: Can we ever take control]

One of the keys to life is to learn self-mastery: to deeply understand what drives you, what frustrates you, and what moves you; you want to be the master of your domain. Like achieving mastery in any subject, self-mastery requires you to become highly educated about yourself. What we know about ACEs suggest that many childhood experiences impact us in adulthood, but we often don't connect the dots. Because we don't connect the dots, we tell people, "This is who I am, and I can't change." So much for self-mastery. But if we look back constructively and identify where we came from, we open our capacity to grow.

[handwritten: Memories]

We often repeat this phrase in our work: it's not *who* you are; it's the *way* you are. In other words, it's how you've been trained. There's a delta between who you are at your core, versus how you arrived at your current behavior. Once you can create space to recognize the difference, you can make conscious choices about what you do and don't want to do. Whether that means you're going to take better care of yourself, stop drinking, cultivate more authentic relationships, pursue your own passions as opposed to the ambitions that other people want for you—all of those choices come by opening up the possibility that growth and change are critical to who you are, and you have the freedom to pursue those goals.

Understanding is the first step toward achieving this freedom; disclosure is the second step. Disclosure is what starts to open up that space needed between how you behave currently, and who you want to be. When you're holding on to something that hasn't been disclosed, it's hard to get over it. You may have identified the source of your struggle, but without naming that out loud in the company of empathetic listeners, it remains stuck inside you.

Imagine a computer with a clogged hard drive. It's still working, but your operating speed and the computer's overall functionality is seriously compromised. Let's identify the computer as your life, and the hard drive as your inner self. We hope by now that we've made it abundantly clear that you don't want to just ignore the issues with your hard drive; unless you want to live the rest of your life with serious limitations, you need to research the hard drive to understand what is causing so many challenges.

So let's say you run a diagnostic test and come up with all sorts of results. There are viruses, unnecessary cookies, apps you don't need, and numerous other issues slowing your hard drive down. Now, do you stop there? Would there be any point in simply identifying what's wrong, without taking the additional step of deleting some of that bad content? Of course not. You've taken the time to understand the issues; now, you need to proactively remove them. In essence, disclosure is what clears the hard drive.

The stakes of failing to do this are high, because other people are depending on you to get well. Research proves that you're at risk of doing to yourself and others what was done to you—and we've seen this play out time and again. Many people who were sexually abused, abuse somebody else. People who grew up in alcoholic households end up being alcoholics; people raised with passive-aggressive communication styles become passive-aggressive, and so on.

These reactions don't always produce bad results; if you grew up with two parents in service-related professions who were passionate about what they did, then you may insist on doing work that you're passionate about: not a bad thing. Alternately, if you grew up in a household where the approval of other people was more important than your own approval, you may pursue a life that ultimately leads to profound personal dissatisfaction.

In the middle of these two default reactions is balance. The person with alcoholic parents may choose to drink, or may choose not to, but drinking doesn't become laden with judgment, control, and power issues. Your behavior is influenced by your past experience until you draw a clear line and make a conscious choice to look it in the face and say, "That's not for me. That's not who I am. I can move forward in a different direction."

How do you draw that clear line in the sand?

We're so glad you asked. We're about to walk you through the activity that we use when helping people obtain a fuller understanding of both the gifts and traumas from their pasts.

BUT FIRST: JOSH'S PEP TALK

It's likely that you may be feeling a great deal of discomfort and a reluctance to go any further. That's normal. In fact, in the many times that we've walked people through a close examination of their past, we've never seen anybody who is eager to look back. That may be the best clue possible to suggest why it's so important. People get incredibly uncomfortable about not wanting to turn over that rock—in many ways, it's easier: "Ignorance is bliss." Either people don't want to look back because the past was difficult, or they don't want to look back because they think it wasn't a big deal.

Many people have suggested to me before that my past doesn't sound like a big deal. When I'm working with military folks as a civilian, they sometimes look at my story and question how "so little" could create so much of an issue. But it did, right? And in order to get to a healthy place, I still had to grapple with it and move through it.

I think, in many ways, trauma is relative to your capacity to deal with it. Your past may be full of easily visible trauma, or the pain you carry may have arisen out of more subtle circumstances. Either way, it holds a power over you until you begin to understand it.

When we struggle, when we're uncomfortable—that's where growth is possible. If it was easy, it wouldn't be worth doing. So let's get on with doing this valuable work.

MY OLD STORY

During our program we conduct at our retreats, we walk people through an exercise to take a good hard look at what we call "My Old Story." Although some therapy exercises focus mainly on the hardships a person experienced when examining the past, we push people to look at their gifts as well. When you look at the gifts that emerged out of your painful experiences, you can balance both sides of the equation, and fight the temptation to cast blame and assume the dreaded victim posture.

We begin by handing our program participants a large piece of paper on which they create a family tree. We call it the M.O.S., which stands for "My Old Story." Beneath the representation of their grandparents, parents, siblings, and any other relevant figures, we have our participants draw themselves and their own family. You can access a copy of this M.O.S. family tree chart on our website, strugglewell.com.

Once people fill in all the labels with the appropriate names, we give them blue pens. Using those blue pens, people start to write down the gifts they received from the people in their tree: "sense of humor;" "love of music;" "work ethic;" "financial knowledge."

Then, using a red pen, participants note anywhere there were Adverse Childhood Experiences: abuse physically, sexually, or verbally; substance abuse; neglect; divorce, and so on. They also write in red anything challenging that family members (including themselves) had to experience or endure, such as extreme poverty. Consistently, the M.O.S. starts to become very red. There's always a mix though. Next to "Grandfather," there may be written in red, "alcoholic," but written in blue, "strong work ethic." You can get gifts from the same people who also passed down traumas, and our lives are living proof.

At the bottom of this chart is written the participant's own name, and if appropriate, their spouse and children. Right above that, we'll hand out a green marker, and we ask participants to draw a green line, dividing their own family from the rest of their family above. We have them draw that line over and over again, until it gets nice and thick. Then we go around and look at each one of them in the eyes. We say, "Now it's your turn to stop it."

We're going to say the same thing to you.

It's your turn to *stop it*.

If you don't stop this multi-generational trauma from continuing on at this point in your life, your children are going to be drawing red around you in ten or fifteen years. Is that the person you want to be? Is that the legacy you want to leave?

Guilt

Un avoidable? Unrealistic?

In the years of watching that exercise play out, that seems to be the turning point for almost everybody. Nobody wants the answer to that question to be "yes." A Marine came to us once who was drinking a bottle of vodka a day. We did this exercise with him and asked him: are you going to put your kids in a situation where they're drawing red around you? He told us, "I'm done." The next week we got a call; he hadn't had a drink. The next month we got a call; he hadn't had a drink. He finally realized that he did have a choice to live differently.

After people complete their M.O.S.—which, in itself, is a mechanical process—we have each person share their

"Old Story" out loud. It's this step of disclosure that begins to move the "head" understanding, depicted on the piece of paper, into an internalized "heart" understanding. Information comes out when they're discussing their family history that may not have been written down, and memories come back. We know that ACEs block a person from deeply tapping into their emotional center—it's those experiences that create debris between a person's head and heart. When each person chooses to share their "Old Story," they look back and start to clear that path.

Once they finish, we have them walk a labyrinth so that they have time to meditate on what emerged, and have the opportunity to let go of their negative experiences and pain. Then, we gather around a fire. Each participant identifies one concrete change that they want to make, in moving forward into their new story. At that point, their rolled-up M.O.S. is put into the fire and burned.

Think about how you might do this in your network of your closest three to five friends. If this is too uncomfortable for you, you should consider working directly with a therapist to better understand and most importantly, disclose your past. Your new story starts now.

NEXT STEPS
REFERENCE THE PAST, AS NEEDED

After completing this exercise, some next steps are usually apparent. First, in order to avoid passing trauma on to your own children, you may need to make some hard decisions, like the Marine who determined he needed to quit drinking. Don't pass on this generational trauma. Do what you need to do to stop the cycle.

Consider once again the car analogy we've talked about several times. Your past is still there in the rearview mirror, and occasionally it's worth glancing at for a lot of reasons. It reminds you how you *don't* want to treat others; it reminds you of what you want to drive away from.

CONTINUE TO SHARE YOUR STORY

You also need to begin having more adult conversations with the people most involved. You need to talk to your kids about breaking the cycle; you need to talk to your spouse or best friend about how you got to where you are, and how you want to change. You need to get real with the people in your three-to-five support network about what you've learned about yourself, and how you need their support to move forward.

In addition to these conversations, it's also important to continue the process of disclosure. We have our program participants start the process at our retreat centers, but all of them need to continue that process once they go home—and the goal is to do so in a way that brings strength and hope to others.

It's by sharing your story that you're able to let it go. It's liberating to cast off shame, guilt, fear, and sadness, and face up to your demons among friends. That's what finally helps you move forward, and take back control over your own life. No longer are you controlled by what happened in your past, but, by the way you want to live. We discuss much more about how to go about healthy disclosure in Chapter Four.

KEEP THE PATH CLEAR

If you've completed your M.O.S. and shared that aloud in the company of empathetic listeners, then you've done some huge work in clearing the debris between your head and your heart. You've enabled yourself to tune into your emotional core, to tap into your deepest-held values, and live in a manner that reflects who *you* desire to be.

Now, it's critical that you engage in practices that allow you to keep that path clean, and maintain that connection. How?

Cultivate Wellness Practices. Unfortunately, we live in

a society where it's far more common to deal with stress and anxiety using unhealthy coping strategies—but don't go back there! If you've read through Chapter Two, you should be on your way to finding healthy practices that lead to wellness and self-regulation. You won't be the only one in your guitar class who's looking to grow through struggle. When you talk to people who have taken up practices like meditation or yoga, you find that, for many of them, their arrival there was preceded by a traumatic event. Something forced them to look elsewhere. Within these wellness pursuits, you'll find others with similar stories of struggle, who are finding positive ways to strengthen themselves.

Remember: struggle continues to come; that's guaranteed. But you can do some preventative work by understanding what works well for your system on the front end. Get yourself stabilized with good people, doing good things for yourself, so that when struggle hits, you have space to respond. Additionally, you've now developed an understanding of how you got here, and have cleared the debris behind you. With the road map of your old story, and all the understanding it represents, you've freed yourself to understand how best to get unstuck when new challenges hit.

Cultivate your network. You can march forward and keep your path clear by surrounding yourself with good people who push you to stay on your path. The best friends in life force you to be true to yourself. When you get thrown off course, they'll help you back on it. When you're out of line or doing something that's inconsistent with who they know you are, they hold you accountable. One of the great aspects of the military community is this intolerance of hypocrisy; they don't suffer fools lightly, and won't hold back in calling you out. Those are the kinds of friends you want—friends who love you, listen well, and hold you accountable. In addition, you may need to prune some toxic relationships out of your life—even if those people are currently close to you. This is also discussed in greater detail in Chapter Four.

Cultivate compassion. The journey of Posttraumatic Growth is not a straight line, and when you hit new challenges, there are times you continue to lean toward blaming others for your current struggles. Every time you struggle to believe you have inherent worth, you may grapple with anger toward your parents who raised you to believe you were only loved conditionally. Every time you doubt your ability to succeed, you might churn over memories of the verbal abuse that was drummed into you as a child.

Do what you can in those moments to once again find compassion for the people who wronged you. We all leave our childhood with some scars—and that's okay. That's not our parents' fault; they did the best they could with the tools and training that they had. You have to forge ahead without blaming people and without becoming a victim. Don't judge yourself, and don't judge the people around you; simply cultivate understanding. Awareness and compassion bring you back to a place where you can remember who you are and how you got there. With a healthy perspective, you can make conscious choices about how to move forward.

Cultivate purpose. When you accept the label of a victim, you rob yourself of power. Ask the important question: "Why?" Not, "Why me?" That's the major difference between walking around with a black cloud over you, and achieving freedom in your life. "Why me?" is superficial and creates a victim mentality. But the question of "Why?" reminds you that this struggle presents you with an opportunity for deeper understanding, and greater strength.

LIVE CONGRUENTLY

We define congruency as a place where your thoughts, feelings, and actions are aligned in a positive manner. And let us emphasize "positive." If you're thinking about killing someone, and feeling like killing someone, and then you go commit murder, that's congruency, but it's far from positive. However, if you have done the hard work to develop your core values, and allow your actions to reflect the deep principles inside you, you'll end up in a positive space.

Congruency has to happen in your life. Otherwise, the honesty and openness you achieve during disclosure doesn't do anybody any good. If your actions don't follow a change in your thoughts and feelings, you continue to put yourself and the people you love at risk. You may decide you want to stop drinking, but if you don't actively take steps to achieve that priority, you remain stuck. The first step was to get your thoughts and feelings out on the table by disclosing the story of your past. Now, it's up to you to go and perform. You need to *act* in a manner that shows your changed thoughts and feelings. We'll help you do that in Chapter Five of this book.

Guides can be helpful in getting you there. Seek out people whose lives you recognize as being congruent. Don't work on the financial area of your Wellness Triangle with a financial manager who's severely in debt. Don't work on your physical health with a personal trainer who's clearly not fit. Who do you know whose life is principled, balanced, and healthy? Does that person live in such a way that consistently reflects his or her values? Seek out that person as you push to make your own life more congruent.

Once your thoughts, feelings, and actions are aligned, you're able to live a congruent lifestyle that people respect and seek to emulate. You become the kind of person that others want in their three-to-five network.

A FLOURISHING SOUL AND SPIRIT

2/8 invoke people

These steps—looking back, disclosure, surrounding your-self with good people, engaging in wellness practices, accepting permission to struggle—collectively serve to give you back the keys to your own kingdom. Your past may have bound you to react in ways that did not reflect the person you ever wanted to be. But freedom from that enables you to enter a world of joy, presence, peace, calm, and connectivity. You can be a congruent human being, one who is able to make conscious choices about how to move forward.

The treasure that comes from connecting your head and your heart is ultimately a connection to your soul. You're opened to consider a world of virtues that may have been too much of a luxury to consider before, when you were simply surviving. These innate qualities can become pil-lars of your new story, such as love, compassion, bliss, non-judgment, and clarity. That clarity gives you the capacity to find and pursue the things that you're passion-ate about, including your purpose and your connection to other human beings.

When you're choosing who you want to be, you're not

a victim of your circumstances anymore. You may find yourself in a situation where something is bothering you, but—unlike before—you are able to understand *why* it bothers you and what you need to do about it. No longer are you making unconscious decisions that were determined by your past; you've made the unconscious, conscious, which means you're now the one shaping your own destiny.

This is what we mean by struggling well. Bad things still happen, but you are in command of yourself. You possess the mental space to respond, rather than react, and can do so with a reservoir of goodwill and strength. Not only are you able to handle new struggles, you can do so in a way that remains positive for the people you care about.

Ultimately, and most significantly, when you clear the debris between your head and your heart, and allow your spirit to flourish, you have the ability to create a new story—one that is authentic, fulfilling, purposeful, and most importantly, true to who you are in the depths of your being.

TAKE A KNEE

You and your team leave before dawn. The mission requires a twelve-mile hike before you reach the staging area. Eight miles in, the desert sun glares, beating down on you and your fellow Soldiers; your eighty-pound pack digs into your shoulders. The team leader calls out, "Take a knee!" With relief, you and the rest of your team drop to a knee. The pause gives you a chance to ease the pressure on your hips and your back. After a rest, your team gets up and continues the hike.

That's what we want for you: we want this pause. We want you to cease your relentless march forward long enough to gather strength in preparation for the trials to come. In some cases, Soldiers are told to repack their bags, and that's what we're telling you to do. Open up your rucksack; examine the heavy weights of your past, and take out what you don't need. The simple act of taking those experiences out of the darkness of your bag and exposing them to the sun makes them a lighter burden to carry. Then, repack. Include the gifts; take what you need. Prepare to continue on your journey smarter, knowledgeable of your mission, mindful of your equipment, more aware of your role, full of understanding about how you will carry out your objective.

During the next mission, you may not have the chance to re-pack your bag—but if you've taken the time to do a thorough inventory now, then you'll know exactly what equipment you're carrying and how to move forward. You won't keep pressing ahead with more and more weight accumulating, until you have to give up. You won't react dangerously in fear when attacked, because you know that you have what you need with you in order to respond with precision and clarity. You won't endanger the people around you; instead, you'll be a force of strength in their midst—of courage, of wisdom, of help. Although the road may get harder ahead, you'll be stronger when you meet it. You'll be ready.

So take a knee and unpack your past.

CHAPTER FOUR

THE SHAME GAME

———

"Shame cannot survive being spoken. It cannot survive empathy."[15]

—BRENÉ BROWN

For more than 2,000 days, he was tortured. The North Vietnamese Soldiers ignored the POW conventions, and instead treated the seized American like a war criminal. Charlie Plumb, captured Naval fighter pilot, found one avenue of freedom within his prison: tapping on his cell wall in code to communicate with the other prisoners.

But it wasn't just the cell walls that stood between Charlie and the other prisoners. Each man there was disconnected from his fellow human beings because of shame. Although the prisoners who had been captured were some of America's finest—trained fighter pilots, physically impressive, enormously intelligent—torture had gotten the best of them.

They knew their instructions: if captured, an American Soldier should provide nothing more than name, rank, serial number, and date of birth. But they'd gone further than that. The relentless agony of torture led them to share more than they'd ever intended.

Each man there came to the realization that he wasn't the man he'd thought he was. Not the best of the best after all—not someone capable of handling anything. Instead, they each had broken under torture, and the space between who they had believed themselves to be, and what they had done, created a gulf of shame. That shame prevented the men from talking to other POWs because they felt unworthy of connection; more importantly, they felt sure they would be exiled from the community.

One night, while tapping on the cell wall to his neighbor in code, Charlie risked a confession. He said, "If you knew what I did, you probably wouldn't want to talk to me. And if you did what I did, I probably wouldn't want to talk to you."

His neighbor asked, "Well, what did you do?"

Charlie owned the truth. "I broke."

Instead of judgment, his neighbor responded with understanding and forgiveness. He said, "There's not a man in this prison who was as strong as he wanted to be."

The truth was, hundreds of men in that prison were all holding on to the same secret; they'd all done the exact same thing. But instead of giving themselves any allowance for breaking under torture, they had each judged themselves harshly.

Yet once someone disclosed the truth, the men were liberated to share honestly. Disconnection was replaced by profound connection; relieved to be fully known and forgiven, the POWs had new energy to encourage one another's strength and survival. Charlie's disclosure didn't just get the weight of secrecy off his own chest; it freed other people from shame and disconnection as well.

SHAME'S ROLE IN THE JOURNEY

On the journey from struggle to strength, there is often one major obstacle in the way of our progress: shame. If not removed, shame can stop you in your tracks and prevent you from achieving the freedom, balance, and peace that you deserve and desire.

Where does the shame come from? For most people, shame either originates in the past, or from unhealthy choices they've made as an adult when reacting badly during times of struggle. Let's look at the first example.

Many hold shame connected to painful experiences from

the past. Consider some of the examples of childhood trauma we've discussed, such as an abused child. Children's understanding of the world is limited to the lens they've been given; if someone hurts a child, and she's told the abuse is somehow her fault, she'll believe that. People who grow up with this kind of history internalize the idea that they're bad at the core. "If I was a good enough kid, my parents wouldn't have gotten divorced." "I wouldn't have gotten abused." "I wouldn't have gotten punished." Shame becomes deeply rooted early in life, and contributes to a belief that you have no value or worth.

This then leads to the second source of shame. As discussed in Chapter Three, when you carry past trauma into adulthood, you may end up committing the same wrongs to others that were done to you. In other cases, you're simply unable to self-regulate, which makes you do things you regret. You get trapped in the React Sine Wave of life where you're not in control; instead, situations dictate your reactions. People describe an inability to remember doing a regrettable act, so strongly was an unconscious behavior triggered. When something bad happens, you may overreact to your present situation—and then must live with the consequences.

Let's say, for instance, that you're struggling in your relationship with your spouse. Your fights contribute to the idea that you have no value, and the combination of fear and sadness that whips up inside you rockets your reaction into rage. So you do something impulsive: you go out, and you cheat on your spouse. Immediately afterwards, you feel terrible. The worthlessness you were battling returns tenfold. Your goal all along was to be a good spouse, a valuable spouse—but now you've only confirmed your worst fears about yourself. The distance between who you want to be, and your actual behavior, spreads further. The shame grows. The sine wave plummets, and the cycle of reaction continues.

This is not what we want for you. In Chapter Three, we walked you through an exercise to share "My Old Story," and we recognize that shame may stand in the way for many of our readers in disclosing that information. That's what we want to address in this chapter.

SHAME LEADS TO DISCONNECTION

Shame's power is rooted in judgment of self. Like the Hanoi Hilton prisoners, shame is born when you recognize that your behavior does not reflect the person you want to be. Recognizing the distance between those two points can create deep self-loathing.

This self-loathing blocks the connection between your head and your heart; the first disconnection happens internally. Let's look at your heart. Perhaps shame has made you feel incompetent or unworthy. Maybe you missed another one of your son's soccer games because you stayed late at work, and you feel like a bad parent. Listening to that shame-message prevents you from effectively functioning in the world, so you cut off those feelings, and deal solely from your head: "He'll get over it. It's me that's paying for his soccer stuff anyway." The source of your compassion, values, and your emotional core is simply cut off.

Often, this makes matters worse, because the distance expands between who you think you are, and the ways you behave. Shame grows. You start to feel as though you're not a good person; you may act out toward your spouse or other loved ones. Your self-confidence, your beliefs, your sense of values erode. You then take that out on the world and on yourself.

Can you see where this is going? An internal disconnection leads to disconnection with other people—and usually that's most apparent with the people you love most. We've discussed in previous chapters that you can't give anything to anyone else that you don't possess yourself. If you possess so much shame that you feel worthless—it's nearly impossible to communicate worth, value, and love to other people.

Unfortunately, the negative consequences of shame don't

stop with relationships. The sense of worthlessness that shame produces makes it nearly impossible to struggle well. How can you build a strong support network if you believe that you're not worthy of good relationships or positive outcomes? How can you identify wellness practices that reflect your values, if you're disconnected from your heart and the source of your values? How can you serve others, if you believe you have nothing to contribute?

IMPORTANCE OF CONNECTION

Standing opposite of shame, is authenticity. People who have authentic relationships in their lives—not just with an intimate spouse, but to the people who surround them—are happier and more fulfilled. Those who can allow themselves to be honestly known experience a healthier relationship with themselves and others. And it's this connection that's the key to a happy, successful, and fulfilling life.

How do we know that? Because the longest running study on the subject of life satisfaction says so.[16]

In 1938, researchers at Harvard began a study that continues to this very day, focused on 268 Harvard sophomores from the years 1939-1944. The study's main goal was to find out what conditions lead to life satisfaction. In essence: what makes us happy? In order to assess this question, participants were tracked in every aspect of their lives—their financial status, their jobs, their relationships, and so on—and were asked to report whether or not they were satisfied in life.

As you might imagine, to attend Harvard at that time meant you were privileged and likely came from substantial means. Critics of the study questioned the results—it seemed obvious that these Harvard students would achieve "life satisfaction," when they had everything going for them. So, in the 1970s, researchers merged the results of the Harvard students with 456 underprivileged men from the inner city of Boston. Critics were appeased and the study has continued to our present day.

What researchers found was clear and indisputable. Whether you grew up in poverty with few opportunities, or at Harvard with many: the key to a happy, healthy, and fulfilling life is *connection to others*. Do you have strong relationships with the people around you? That, according to this decades-long study, was the key to happiness, no matter what your background.

This makes sense when you think about the tribal nature of humanity. In ancient days, the worst punishment a person could receive wasn't death—it was exile. It was isolation from fellow human beings. Military personnel have an easy time recognizing this truth as well; for many, the bond formed with fellow Soldiers is the military's greatest feature.

WHAT KEEPS YOU DISCONNECTED

Unfortunately, even though times of struggle are when you need people the most, it can be these hardest experiences that lead you into a painful self-exile. The story of the Hanoi Hilton illustrates this. Each prisoner thought something was wrong with him uniquely, and was ashamed to admit his struggle or need for help. That same phenomenon exists today. Everyone's struggling and no one wants to be the first to admit it.

Our culture perpetuates this problem. Americans are generally seen as being more divided than ever before, and we spend enormous effort differentiating ourselves from others, whether through politics, gender, race, the views we share on social media, or something else. We work *against* connecting with others because we view them as different, or because we're preoccupied with distractions. In addition to this, the filtered picture of life that we see on social media does nothing to remind us that we're all in this together. We see pictures of what look like perfect lives, and get the impression that we're alone in our struggles. Our "friends" and "followers" count may be in the thousands, but how many relationships are with people who make us feel truly at home?

"That which draws us nearer our fellow man, is that the deep heart in one, answers the deep heart in another."[17]

—RALPH WALDO EMERSON

And yet, we share something foundational with every other human on earth, deep in our soul. The "deep heart" connection identified by Emerson describes the incredible fulfillment experienced when you are fully known and accepted in a relationship. The people who have that deep heart connection report joy, fulfillment, and gratitude, no matter what their material status might be.

Brené Brown, PhD, LMSW, and author of *The Gifts of Imperfection,* is a well-known researcher who has supplied a wealth of findings on this subject. According to her research, there are two things that people require in life, at a base level: love and connection. These two qualities are especially needed during struggle. She found that the difference between people who have love and connection in their lives—people she refers to as "the wholehearted"—and those who don't, is that the "wholehearted" believe they're *worthy* of connection.[18]

"Well, that's great," you might be thinking. "I'm dealing with shame, which makes me feel unworthy. And you're telling me that the only way to be happy is to have good relationships, which means I need to believe I'm worthy. So apparently, I'm going to lead a miserable life." Not so! There's a way to climb out of the shame-cycle, and reclaim self-worth.

STRUGGLE TO STRENGTH

We believe the answer comes back to honesty. Whereas shame leads to disconnection, isolation, and dishonesty—honesty leads to connection.

We say this, again, because we've seen it. We ran one of the first male military sexual trauma programs at our retreat center. The standard perception was (and is) that military sexual assault only happens to females; men supposedly couldn't be victims of sexual assault. Those preconceived notions meant that these guys carried enormous shame, feeling that there was no way for them to disclose their stories. They believed they were each alone in carrying the worst secret ever, and they didn't think anyone else would understand.

However, once the men were gathered and a safe space was established for them to talk openly, the common experience among them made them stronger. Each man realized he wasn't alone in his trauma. As each Soldier disclosed the story that had fueled his shame, the weight visibly lifted off his chest. Their honesty opened a critical door, leading them from solitary confinement to a community where they were known, seen, and respected.

We've heard people share stories of mental health issues, abuse, murder, of having a mother who was a prostitute, of having twelve stepfathers—but when people choose to share their stories together, there is a mutual strengthening that occurs. People realize that everyone has been through major tragedies; everyone has behaved in ways that cause shame. However, that realization doesn't create an impression of weakness; rather, it builds a sense of strength and freedom, when hope returns.

We acknowledge that it takes tremendous risk to go there. And, for many of the people we work with, that's why they haven't gone "there" yet, in dealing with their struggles. Rather than risk acknowledging your shameful moments, it feels easier to play whack-a-mole and focus mainly on what's happening in your immediate present, or to distract yourself with other coping mechanisms. It feels more comfortable to deal with surface-level issues, using surface-level solutions. But here's the thing: this is an inside-out game. If you want to fix the outside, you need to start with the inside. It doesn't work the other way.

And keep in mind, strength follows struggle. We're able to explain this phenomenon to our military folks, because they've already experienced a transition from struggle to strength. When they were brought into the military, their drill instructors took everything they owned. The Soldiers' heads were shaved. Their names were taken away. Nearly every element of who they had known themselves to be was denied them. This was struggle.

But after their identity was stripped down to the basics, they were built up again: piece by piece, layer by layer. They built discipline, principles, and values. Soldiers were taught how to shoot, run, and perform skills they'd never done before. They graduated boot camp and became a Soldier, a Marine, a Sailor, an Airman. This is strength.

This journey doesn't just happen in the military: a new life follows painful childbirth; musical excellence comes after countless hours of practice; a home is built with sweat, toil, and time. And freedom follows disclosure.

"If you can get through to doing things that you hate to do: on the other side is greatness."[19]
—DAVID GOGGINS, NAVY SEAL, ARMY RANGER, AND USAF TACTICAL AIR CONTROLLER, ULTRA-RACE ATHLETE, AND DESCRIBED AS THE "TOUGHEST MAN IN THE WORLD"

This same opportunity to journey from struggle to strength exists again. Now is the time to rise up through the grist of the training and choose a path of strength. This path isn't an easy one, but it's useless to try to take a shortcut around it—the only way out is through. If your foundation is cracked, anything you build on top of it isn't going to hold. That's why you've got to start with your core.

If you dread the thought of doing what it takes to be fully known, that's a clear sign this is one of the most important steps you need to take. With training and with personal fortitude you'll be able to take it.

We want to help you walk this journey. Probably the biggest reason people are reluctant to share is that they hold tremendous self-judgment and fear similar judgment from others. In order to address this particular fear, later on in this chapter we'll get into specific recommendations for how to share well, and what kind of people you need around you in order to share safely, and be received without judgment.

First though, we need to take a closer look at what's happening for all of us underneath the surface.

DEFINITION OF STRUGGLE: INTERNAL TENSION

There's a powerful Cherokee legend that captures the essence of the battle that occurs within all humans—the battle that produces the lion's share of our struggle and tension. It goes like this:

> One evening, an old Cherokee told his grandson about a battle that goes on inside of people. He said, "My son, the battle is between two wolves inside us all. One is evil. It is anger, envy, jealousy, sorrow, regret,

greed, shame, arrogance, self-pity, guilt, resentment, inferiority, lies, false pride, superiority, and ego."

He continued, "The other is good. It is joy, peace, love, hope, serenity, humility, kindness, benevolence, empathy, generosity, truth, compassion, and faith."

The grandson thought about it for a minute and then asked his grandfather, "Which wolf wins?"

The old Cherokee simply replied, "The one you feed."

This parable illustrates our definition of struggle: struggle occurs when there is a deep internal tension between *who* you are and *where* you are. Generally, you want to feed the good wolf; you aspire to be a good person, a role model, and a person who positively influences others. That's *who* you want to be—but that's not where you may end up.

No one wants to feed the evil wolf, and yet all of us sometimes do. And when you feed the evil wolf, you judge yourself five times as harshly as when you feed the good one. You beat yourself up for those failures—which, ironically, can result in you feeding the bad wolf further, deepening your sense of regret, shame, self-pity, guilt, resentment, inferiority, false pride, and so on. That harsh self-judgment then leads to the destructive disconnection we discussed earlier.

And yet—you're human. You're fallible. You have in common the same struggle of every other human. There's internal tension between who you want to be, and how you behave.

You don't need to look any further than our own lives for proof: when Josh was in crisis-mode, it was because the person he portrayed to the outside world—that shiny, nice Wellness Triangle—was vastly different from who he was on the inside, which was a total mess. Ken has experienced this too. Although he recognized his own father as a workaholic, Ken ended up repeating the same pattern with his own family. His deployments, military service, and work ended up keeping him away from his daughters for much of their lives—a pattern he's now trying to correct with his grandchildren. We've experienced firsthand this tension between who we want to be and where we are.

Yet rarely is struggle understood to be so universal. Often when people struggle, they categorize themselves as broken or defective. Labels enter the picture: "I'm depressed." "I have PTSD." Not only does this mean you identify yourself by your worst experiences, you also fail to dig deeper into what might really be going on. What's more, you use this surface explanation as the excuse for all your behaviors. "This is why I don't have any friends. This is why I don't get out of bed. This is why I'm an asshole."

One of the most powerful moments that occurs in our

program is when we ask people, "How many of you have been told there's something wrong with you? How many of you believe it?" They all believe that there's something wrong with them—and are living with the weight of that indictment.

Here's what we know: there's nothing wrong with you. You're simply living out what happened to you, and you need to be retrained. Stop judging yourself and instead, recognize that you're a function of your experiences and your training. From that place, you can move forward productively and constructively. Rather than saying, "I am depressed," admit, "I feel depressed." Feeling depressed might be a description of *where* you are, but it isn't *who* you are. Yes, the tension produced between those two points produces struggle. However, it doesn't define you.

At the end of this parable, the grandfather points out to his grandson that he has a choice to make. All of us have fed both the evil and the good wolf—but now what? We've got to choose how we'll move forward.

Will you continue to feed the evil wolf and engage in secrecy? Will you live in shame and guilt? Will you lie to those you love, to hide the choices you're ashamed of? Will you get defensive and arrogant when your spouse makes a comment about your behavior? Will you fixate on the moments you fed the bad wolf and internalize those mistakes into a belief system that defines you? Will you continue to avoid looking at the person in the mirror?

Or will you make a different choice? Will you have compassion for yourself, choosing to focus on the times when you fed the good wolf? Will you be humble and truthful by willingly choosing to share the moments when you fed the evil wolf? Will you hope for the empathy of others and extend them empathy in turn?

For those who feel stuck in shame, there is only one way forward in choosing the good: disclosure. It is nearly impossible to access the qualities of the good wolf—joy, peace, love, hope, serenity, empathy, compassion, faith—if you cannot extend any of those qualities to yourself, due to shame. And the only way to free yourself from this self-judgment is by speaking your truth, and receiving the forgiveness, compassion, kindness, and empathy of others. It's that experience that enables you to let go of all of the emotions and judgments you've used to indict yourself.

One young woman in our program talked about cheating with some married men, something that she deeply regretted. Yet she described the relief after sharing being like having a wagon unhitched from her chest: that was the magnitude of the weight lifted. In another session, we heard two men share that they had both killed a child in combat. Neither man could forgive himself—but then they talked to each other. One man forgave the other one for what he had done, and then the other man forgave him. Although each man needed and wanted forgiveness, he wasn't able to extend it to himself. They needed it from an external source—and sharing their story enabled them to receive it.

Disclosure is the epitome of emptying the rucksack you carry: the heaviest rocks in there are the ones related to shame. It's those rocks that convince you your struggle isn't something you can change—that you're beyond help, in it because of someone else, or stuck with a victim's label. By emptying out those rocks in the company of an empathetic listener, the weight of shame dissolves. You free yourself to choose to get healthier and make better choices.

Although it might be tempting to simply analyze your past struggles privately, we believe that, without sharing, the shame is never released. The experience of telling your story in the company of people who won't judge you is crucial. You need someone to take the stick away from you that you're using to beat yourself. Furthermore, this process of sharing allows you to deepen your relationships. Dishonesty leads to isolation, but honesty builds trust. Choosing to be this authentic with your three-to-five network leads those relationships into new levels of depth and understanding.

We've talked a lot about disclosure. Now let's talk about how to do it in practice.

CHOOSING TO RECONNECT

In Chapter One, we identified the five domains of Post-traumatic Growth: deeper relationships, personal strength, spiritual/existential change, appreciation for life, and new possibilities. In order to get all those wonderful things, there are five phases a person must go through. We've talked about the first two: education (understanding the value, inevitability, and impact of struggle, and how to live and struggle well) and regulation (staying grounded via your support network and wellness practices). The third phase is disclosure.

Chapter Three walked you through the "My Old Story" exercise to help you discover *what* content to share. Now, we want to discuss more clearly *how* to share. There's a right way and a wrong way to do this; there's also right people and wrong people to do it with. In order to get the most out of this step of disclosure, we want to acquaint you with what we've found to be important ways to do it well.

DISCLOSURE: HOW-TO

The first area discussed in this section addresses you, listing actions that only you can take. The second area focuses on others, helping you identify the kind of people you need in your three-to-five network—the people who can best receive your most loaded stories.

As you read this, keep in mind that we highly recommend *mutual* disclosure. Mutual disclosure builds honesty, trust, and shared strengthening; it's therefore much more valuable to share your story in the company of people who likewise are honest about their own experiences. However, if you realize after reading this section that your network is currently not healthy, then going through the "My Old Story" disclosure exercise with a professional may be your best starting point.

Ideally though? You'd get a couple friends together, go through the "My Old Story" exercise, and then talk through it. You're not aiming for a cry-fest; the goal is to explore your experiences as an observer, so you can achieve greater understanding. We discourage people from "reliving" their experiences, which can be emotionally taxing and even re-traumatizing. Instead, just talk through the facts of what happened and how it's impacted you. Share and listen well to one another. Avoid interrupting, giving advice, or casting judgment.

And keep the following points in mind.

Viktor Frankl writes about the idea that the mental health system treats people like machines in need of repair.[20] This suggestion is counterproductive: the moment people get the idea that they need repair, they are robbed of the power to change themselves.

In one of our sessions recently, we received feedback from a woman at the end of our program. She said, "I got to the airport and I kept waiting for you all to treat me like I was broken. Like I was 'PTSD Jane.' I kept waiting...and waiting. And you didn't do it. You treated me like a friend, like a human being." We had treated Jane the same way we treat everyone who comes through our doors: as the person she can become. That changed her perception of herself, which allowed her to take steps she hadn't been ready to take before.

When you treat everyone as the person they can become—including yourself—they'll aspire to become that. But if you treat them like they *are*—including yourself—you'll lock them in place. Sometimes our own self-judgment has gotten us stuck, which is why a good friend may be needed to speak out that correction: "There's nothing wrong with you. I see you as something more." Chances are, you're able to speak that truth to someone else who's hurting. Can you believe it for yourself?

Some People "Can't Handle the Truth"

In the movie, *A Few Good Men*, a climactic scene depicts Jack Nicholson as a Marine Colonel on the witness stand, being grilled by a Naval lawyer, played by Tom Cruise. Cruise's character demands, "I want the truth!" Jack Nicholson roars back, "You can't handle the truth!"[21]

Unfortunately, this is often the case. Many people can't handle the truth. Imagine walking down the hallway of your workplace, when a coworker asks, "How's it going?" Let's say that you tell her, "Pretty bad. Are you prepared to sit down and listen?" Her eyes widen, she says, "Oh, I'm sorry..." And then provides an excuse to get back to her desk.

If you were to call after her, "You can't handle the truth!"— you'd be right.

When people ask you how you're doing, and you're honest about being in the midst of struggle—some people run for the hills. We've experienced this firsthand, as Josh's story below can attest. In those instances, that run-away-response is typically an indication that those people are struggling with something similar and doing their best to avoid dealing with it. Their response isn't so much a judgment on you, as it is revealing about them.

Our advice? Be honest anyway.

JOSH'S STORY: CHANNELING JACK NICHOLSON AND MILEY CYRUS

I remember a moment standing at a vineyard in France, just after my divorce was finalized, looking at this beautiful mountainside of vines. It hit me that I wasn't okay—I was in a really bad place. I resolved right then, that whenever anyone asked me how I was doing, I would tell them the truth.

So I tried it. When I came back and people asked me how I was, I'd admit, "I'm not good at all. I'm a complete mess." People didn't like hearing that. Some of my closest friends encouraged me to stop sharing with them and pursue counseling instead. But the people I saw in the mental health world weren't helpful; they didn't listen or share.

One day I was staying with a friend, and he told me that I had to watch an interview with Miley Cyrus on Ellen DeGeneres' show. I started watching it and I was dumbfounded. Here was someone in the public eye, constantly being scrutinized and criticized, and she insisted on going her own way and figuring out who she truly was. Miley provided me with the inspiration I needed and a new slogan: what other people thought of me was none of my business. I decided that I would stick to my guns and remain open, honest, and insistent on sharing my truth. Eventually, I *did* find people that could handle the truth.

I worked for a guy named Mort who was no stranger to

tragedy—he had lost his son at a young age. One day, I told him, "I'm not okay, Mort. I'm in a really bad place."

He looked at me and he said, "You are. And that's okay." He continued, "It will probably take you three months to three years to get through this. But you will get through it. And I want you to know that I don't care where you work or what you do, I just want you to be happy." That was a pivotal moment for me. Mort didn't try to argue with me, or fix me—he simply acknowledged that what I said was true. And provided me with a healthy dose of hope and support.

Other people were able to handle the truth—people I had underestimated. I remember having lunch with various friends I had known for a number of years. As I sat with them and shared my story, nearly every single one opened up to me in turn. I thought I knew some of these people well—but it turned out I didn't know them at all. I discovered that people have enormous depths that they don't often reveal, and we only gain access to it by exposing our own depth. One of the more beautiful experiences that I had during a dark time was deepening my relationships.

Choosing to share, even knowing that you might experience rejection, enables you to deepen your connections with people already in your life. Some of our acquaintances are amazing people—but discovering that requires getting to that next level of depth with them. The people who can handle the truth are the ones who have made peace with their own stories. Those are people you want around.

Share the Deep Truth

"Above all, don't lie to yourself. The man who lies to himself and listens to his own lie comes to a point that he cannot distinguish the truth within him, or around him, and so loses all respect for himself and for others. And having no respect, he ceases to love."[22]

—FYODOR DOSTOYEVSKY

Here's a way you might try to shortcut your way through shame: you tell the truth, but not the whole truth. Or you tell an "amended" truth that makes you feel better about your role in a given experience. As Dostoyevsky points out though, when you lie to yourself about what happened, that doesn't liberate you from shame—that deepens shame. When you can be honest with yourself, you can be honest with other people. This honesty is the only way you experience greater self-awareness and a release from what weighs you down.

This "whole truth" is something we call the "deep truth." How do you know if you're sharing the deep truth? When people are encouraged to share at a twelve-step meeting, there's a common idea that if you don't remember what you said, then you shared deeply. In essence, the goal is to get beyond your head's inhibitions, and share from a place deep within you. You share the things that you don't want to share.

For people seeking congruence in their thoughts, feelings, and actions, there must be a willingness to share the deep stuff. It's far too convenient to only share your thoughts when you're on the mountain top, reveling in triumph. How did you get there? How can others get there? In order to help yourself and others walk this journey, you need to share when you're suffering in the valley as well.

Accept and Give Permission to Struggle

If our Facebook-and-Instagram-filtered-society tells us anything, it's that we're supposed to portray a seamless, effortless, successful life. But if that's the case, then we don't have the freedom to talk about the days when we're struggling. Attempts to do that on social media often rocket to the far side of the spectrum, like when people voice suicidal thoughts or deep depression to an impersonal digital network. Where's the balance?

People desperately need permission to be human, to have their own sine waves go up and down. If we give ourselves permission to be true about what's going on in our lives, we are set free, and can help others find that same freedom. Part of achieving congruence in life requires living with this authenticity: if you're having a terrible day, but act as though everything's fine, you're not congruent. You're faking it, rather than allowing people to witness your honest struggle.

But you don't have to fake it anymore. You've had the courage to do something that the majority of people refuse to do—you've looked back. You've built an awareness of why you struggle with what you do and what happened in your past. You've disclosed that story and reconnected your head and your heart. You've set yourself on a course to get your thoughts, feelings, and your actions all aligned. You can be real; you have that permission.

When you accept this permission to move forward, without self-judgment or judgment from others, you're able to deepen your relationship with yourself and other human beings. How many times in your life have you reflected on who you are, without any judgment? Yet that's what accepting this permission affords you. You gain deep insight into who you are, and a profound sense of acceptance. *It's okay* that you're having a hard time.

Even more significantly, you're able to stop perpetrating fear and sadness in the lives of the people around you. Before you made the choice to examine and disclose the story of your past, your actions may have been primarily driven by fear or sadness. In either instance, you're a negative influence on the people around you, often taking your pain out on them—or yourself. Freeing yourself from these binding ties means you have the opportunity to serve as a positive influence in a world that desperately needs more compassionate people being real.

IDENTIFY THE SUPERFICIAL, THE TOXIC, AND THE GOOD

We've talked about points you need to keep in mind when sharing your story. We want to address now the people you choose to share with. It's likely that the people in your extended network of acquaintances are going to fall into one of three categories: the superficial relationships, the toxic ones, and the people you want in your three-to-five network.

Superficial Relationships

Superficial relationships deal with life on a surface level—and it's okay to have these superficial connections. Sometimes those friends bring out the most fun. Maybe they don't help you achieve the most happiness or deep joy, but their presence in your life may still be valuable. Sometimes, it's great to just go bowling with a bunch of guys that could care less about what you're going through, and enjoy sharing beers and chicken wings. It makes for a good night.

It's likely that when your struggle intensifies, these super-ficial friendships wouldn't be the first people you choose to share with. That's a valuable thing to recognize. The goal is to ultimately identify your network of close friends for when you *do* have the need for deep listeners. There's a time and a place for your "fun" friends—although it is necessary to develop some relationships that accommo-date much greater depth.

Toxic Relationships and Pruning

Some people in your life may simply be toxic, and those are relationships you may need to cut out of your life, either temporarily or permanently—a step we call "pruning." We believe very strongly that you become the average of the three to five people you spend the most time with. If any of those five people are toxic, and you don't prune them out of your life, their negative influence persists. That goes for family members too, and may even present the possibility of divorce. If you're in an unhealthy or judg-mental community, you may need to move out of your community. Drastic changes might be required.

Perhaps this sounds extreme, but we believe you can't help anybody else in this world until you are healthy. Toxic people are often in need of help themselves. It takes extreme personal wellness to be able to love people for who they are deep in their souls, and not blame them for the harm they might be doing to themselves or others—especially if you are at risk of absorbing some of that harm. You are not able to help a toxic person, until you become healthy yourself. To do that, you need to get around three to five people that help get you right and keep you right. You need to get your regulation practices in place and put yourself on a healthy trajectory.

Pruning doesn't mean you cut people out of your life with no compassion; if anything, we hope walking people through the "My Old Story" exercise helps *build* compassion. The people in your family tree who inflicted pain on you were more often than not repeating what was done to them. With this in mind, it's appropriate and even necessary for your own healing to consider those people with compassion. However, mix that compassion with a sense of space in order to do what's safe and healthy for you. You can't walk around your whole life blaming other people for how you are or what you're doing—but you can identify that there are people who may be toxic for you at given points in time.

If you recognize a relationship is toxic when doing the "My Old Story" exercise, first you need to get healthy yourself—which may require stepping away from that person or people. Sometimes we need distance to achieve clarity about which people most deserve our time and energy. If you can't be healthy because of what's surrounding you, then you need to change your surroundings.

After pruning a person from your life, it may eventually be appropriate to pursue reconciliation with them, along with new boundaries that you've identified after getting healthier. In a more stable place, your understanding of your relationships may change; it may be that what shifts isn't the nature of the relationship, but your perspective of that other person, along with your capacity to be kind and empathetic. Sometimes, the other person can adapt and respond to that, and you can enjoy a fresh start. But if the other person is unwilling to relate to you as a healthier individual, you may need to prune them out of your life entirely.

We've experienced both versions of this. While going through his divorce, Josh asked his parents for some distance so that he had the space he needed to better understand what he wanted to do. After getting to a healthier place, he's now back in regular contact with them. Ken has pruned some of his family out of his life entirely. It's been clear that those relationships will always remain toxic, and he's decided it's more important at this stage in his life to invest his time and energy into his four grandkids.

You prune back a rosebush in order to help increase the plant's growth. After stepping away from unhealthy relationships, you can obtain the stability and clarity you need to determine what's necessary for future growth. Do you prune a branch, and then burn it? Or do you prune a branch so that it can regrow in a healthier manner? Getting some distance may be necessary to make these types of decisions. The end goal is to become healthier yourself, so that you can love others in your life with compassion, empathy, and without judgment.

Strategies for Building Your Support Network

At this point in the chapter, you should be able to assess the quality of your relationships with the three to five people you spend the most time with. Do any of those relationships need to be deepened beyond a superficial level? Do any of those people need to be pruned from your life? And if you've recognized the hard reality that some of those three to five people should not be in your closest network—who do you replace them with?

If you recognize deficits in your current network of closest relationships, consider again what kind of person you most need in your three to five. You want to find good, empathetic listeners, who are there for you when you need them. These people should be healthy people whose lives you respect, people trying to be better versions of themselves. In their company, you're allowed to be authentic—and in fact, they insist upon you being so. If and when you revert back to unhealthy habits, these are people who remind you of who you're ultimately trying to be, and hold you accountable.

JOSH'S STORY: THE ONE WHO WASN'T A SHIT-BAG

After my divorce, I did the not-so-original thing of trying to regain some confidence by sleeping around. In this phase, I had accumulated a group of single guys who were, in military terms, shit-bags. They were not good people. I remember bragging to a friend outside of this group about these sexual conquests as if I was a college sophomore—even though I was much older than that and definitely knew better. My friend said, "Hey, dude. At some point, I think you're going to have to re-find your moral compass."

That was a wake-up call.

His words reminded me how much I valued him as a friend. He told me what was true even though I'm sure it was hard—and it reminded me that I needed to take a long, hard look at what I was doing and the people I was surrounded by.

At that time, I was trying to pick up the pieces of my life, but I was doing it blind. It's like I was looking at the back of a puzzle, and all I could see was the brown cardboard. But when we have great people in our lives—like this friend who called me out—those people can see what the face of the puzzle looks like, and how it's meant to be completed. They push us, hold us accountable, and support us to become the version of ourselves they know we can be.

Some people think kindness means you never say anything another person doesn't want to hear—but that's not true. People who love you, value you, and believe in you, sometimes show you the deepest kindness by voicing the hard truth. You need those voices in your life. Our motto is: say what you mean, mean what you say, and don't say it mean.

Finding Your People

We've described the kind of person you want in your three-to-five network. If you don't already have people like that on your speed-dial, then consider: is there anyone in your immediate or extended network that *does* fit the bill? Get lunch with that person. Take a class with that person. Start taking up some of the habits you see that person practicing. It's rare that somebody doesn't have at least one person that can launch them into a healthier network—so start there.

If you recognize that what you're doing isn't working to create the life you want, then you've got to change what you're doing. Pursuing wellness practices can aid in this, as we mentioned in Chapter Two. If you're looking to improve your physical health and sign up for a spin class, you'll encounter a new group of people. Get to know your instructors and fellow classmates—they're all people who share at least one value with you and might hold potential for real depth. If you want to deepen your mental wellness, join a book club, or art group, or a lecture series. These groups could lead to authentic conversations about inspiration or deeper meaning. As you pursue new practices, you'll encounter other people who have found grace and joy in similar ways.

Also, don't look *past* your current network. Rather than assuming that the people in your current network will only ever engage with you on a superficial level, try to initiate deeper conversations with them—see where those go. People have layers; you may only know their outer shell, but that doesn't mean there isn't plenty to discover under the surface. If you take the risk to share honestly with others, you might be surprised by who follows.

Finally, keep in mind that successful, quality relationships still experience struggle. Expect that. You can assume that any couple celebrating their fiftieth anniversary has had to work through their fair share of challenges, but they committed for the long haul. Whether it's a marriage or a friendship, it takes hard work and honest communication to make a successful relationship last.

Recently, some challenges arose in our organization that weren't being discussed, and tension was coming out in negative ways. We sat down for three hours with our staff and talked with them deeply and honestly. Everyone spoke from the heart and showed that they were willing to listen well. It was a beautiful thing to experience—to know that we were among people who were going to say what was on their mind and heart, and do so kindly. They were able to honestly voice their needs in the presence of people who listened intently.

Those are the kinds of connections we're striving for. In successful relationships, struggle can make the relationship deeper, if both parties lean into it. We accept the fact that the only way out is through, and if you attempt to go around a conflict rather than through it, you'll miss the opportunity to achieve deeper understanding with the people you love. It's hard work, true—but so is everything else worth doing.

OUR CHALLENGE TO YOU

You may have thought this section was only going to be about other people—but assembling your network is a step that *you* need to take. It is your job to do the soul-searching required to evaluate your closest relationships and find new ones, if necessary. Yes, this might be hard; it might result in some awkward or uncomfortable moments. But this step is nonnegotiable. It's absolutely crucial to build a strong network if you want to struggle well.

As you build your network, continue to do the hard work

of getting healthy yourself. We've spoken about the tremendous value of relationships, but don't use that as an excuse to get into a codependent relationship. If you don't find yourself with an internal sense of self-worth, it can be tempting—but ultimately ineffective—to find that worth outside of yourself. Sometimes this includes getting into relationships with people that make you feel good for a little while...until they don't. You might try to chase money, fame, or other temporary mechanisms to attach your self-worth to, but when the good feeling runs out, you're back where you started.

Connect your head and your heart to understand who you are; then, bring that understanding into your relationships with other people. That's the way to authenticity; that's the way to meaningful relationships that are mutually beneficial.

LET GO AND FREE YOURSELF

By making peace with your past and dealing with your shame, you're liberated to recognize that there's nothing wrong with you! These experiences haven't impacted you in some permanent way, and you can retrain yourself to move beyond them. By looking your past square in the face and bringing it into the light, you're able to rob it of its power to unconsciously control you and instead, make it useful.

Keep in mind the areas enhanced through Posttraumatic Growth. Not only do you experience greater personal strength, spiritual and existential change, appreciation for life, and new possibilities—your relationships are also made deeper through greater compassion and empathy. This last gift is made possible by the *work* required to achieve Posttraumatic Growth. Deep relationships require disclosure.

We've acknowledged the fear people might possess in facing the past and choosing disclosure. But remember: "the cave you fear to enter holds the treasures that you seek."[23] The treasures truly worth finding are intangible. They're gifts like deep relationships, an understanding of what truly matters in life, connection with others, gratitude for the small things, enjoyment of nature, and a sense of strength that you can do anything.

We've experienced these treasures through our own hard-fought journeys and can attest that the road through struggle is worth traveling. It's the most beautiful, majestic, and fulfilling journey you will ever undergo. And once you've made it, you can help other people find that cave full of treasures too.

KEN'S STORY: CLEARING THE MINEFIELD

In my work as a bomb disposal specialist, I had to clear

minefields. When you confront a minefield, you have a couple options. The first, and easiest, is to simply walk around the minefield or fly over the field in a helicopter. The problem with this option is that you don't make travel through that area safe for anyone following you. More often, my job was to clear a safe path for others to follow.

It may sound strange to people who aren't in my profession, but most landmines in the ground are not a big deal, so long as you don't step on them. You can literally pick them up and carry them away to a safe disposal area. But every so often, we'd run into something much more dangerous.

I remember one nasty stretch in Bosnia. We were literally on our hands and knees clearing these mines when we found sophisticated booby traps lying underneath. Some minefields are just set up as a defensive measure, but this field was an aggressive attempt to take out anyone crossing it or disarming it. The people who set it up deliberately wanted to prevent anyone's forward progress.

We'd hit a mine, start to dig it up, and then find another mine underneath it, or a hand grenade with a pin pulled, or a tripwire attached. If we hadn't dug under those mines deeply enough, we would have been destroyed. But once we identified there was a bigger threat than just that single landmine laying on the ground, we knew that every mine we came up to required extra attention and a little more clearance underneath to make it safe.

Sometimes we didn't blow them up because we were working covertly in the middle of the night. In those cases, we marked them so everybody could see the hazards in their night vision goggles and go around them. We did what we needed to do to get people from point A to point B as quickly and safely as possible. That field in particular required a ton of work—but we learned plenty of new strategies about how to deal with the next one.

Here's my point: in life, you're going to confront a lot of minefields. Those fields of struggle are going to regularly be dropped in your path, and they'll do everything they can to prevent you from moving forward. Each mine is set and buried by events in your past, and can be easily triggered by events in your present if they're not dug up.

Sure, you could just ignore the problem, and try to go around or over it—like hopping in a helicopter and simply flying over the minefield. But doing that teaches you nothing about handling the next stretch of struggle. You also don't do anything to help the people who are relying on you to clear a safe path, like your loved ones. The better option for yourself and for others is to go through it and deal with the danger.

By building up an understanding of what kind of debris you're personally carrying, you'll know what approach to use in dealing with new struggles. Some problems in our lives can be dealt with superficially—you can simply identify the mine, pick it up, and carry it away. Or, you mark it for the people following you, so that they know how to navigate around it.

Other problems connect to danger much deeper within us. It's not just the mine that could be triggered on the surface; there are booby traps underneath, which require deep digging to remove. Those problems necessitate a lot more time and energy to solve—but those are also the fields that teach you the most about getting through the next minefield of struggle.

We want to stress here that even when dealing with a minefield, you have a choice. You can choose how best to deal with it, and you can access different strategies for clearing the mines. However, this choice *only* comes through building your understanding of what's there. If you don't acknowledge the danger in front of you, or the danger buried within you, then you don't have a choice. You'll trigger these explosives, hurting yourself and others.

Clear the path between your head and heart of shame, guilt, trauma, and self-judgment. With your head and your heart connected, you exude authenticity, truth, love, and empathy. From that place, you have the opportunity to decide how you want to train yourself for the next phase of your life, which is creating and living your new story.

In this new story, you're allowed to make mistakes, to realize that even though you may fail, you are not a failure. You have the opportunity to let go of judgment and to stop being your own worst enemy. As you learn to show empathy to others, you learn to be kind, honest, and empathetic with yourself. No longer are you a prisoner of your own mind; you're free.

CHAPTER FIVE

CREATING AND LIVING YOUR NEW STORY

———

"For what it's worth: it's never too late or, in my case, too early to be whoever you want to be. There's no time limit, stop whenever you want. You can change or stay the same, there are no rules to this thing. We can make the best or the worst of it. I hope you make the best of it. And I hope you see things that startle you. I hope you feel things you never felt before. I hope you meet people with a different point of view. I hope you live a life you're proud of. If you find that you're not, I hope you have the courage to start all over again."[24]

—ERIC ROTH, *THE CURIOUS CASE OF BENJAMIN BUTTON*

JOSH'S STORY: A CENTENARIAN'S RESOLUTION

When my grandmother was 100, I sat down with her and

asked to hear some of the wisdom she'd collected after a century of living. I still have the recording of that conversation—it contains snippets like, "When you love what you do, you'll wake up every morning and be excited to go do it." Or, "If you pick the right person, the lights go on every time they walk into a room."

It's not those sage bits of advice that have stuck with me most after that time with my grandmother though—it was her determination to always keep evolving and growing that truly amazed me. When she was ninety, soon after my grandfather (her husband of sixty years) passed, she made a conscious choice. She told me about her decision ten years later: "Your grandfather was such a kind man, and a good man. I realized that I should have been nicer to him. So I've made a commitment that for the rest of my life, I'm going to be really nice to people." My grandmother passed away in October 2017, just six weeks shy of her 103rd birthday. I'll be damned if the last twelve years of her life weren't filled with kindness, gratitude, joy, and love, just as she promised. At 101, she took her first meditation class. And only three weeks before she passed away, we discussed the classes she had signed up for at her assisted living home, and her insistence on being a lifelong learner.

If my grandmother has shown me anything, it's that it's never too late to change. At any moment in our lives, we are presented with the opportunity to choose who we become. We have the choice to look at our old story and decide that's not my movie anymore. It's time to rewrite the script and create a new story. It doesn't matter what age you are, or how much you've been through. "It's never too late or too early to be whoever you want to be."

Through making peace with your past and understanding yourself, you're able to develop a deep wisdom about who you are, what you care about, and who you want to become. For possibly the first time, you have the opportunity to make conscious choices about how you'd like to shape your own destiny. You can choose to remain the same, or you can choose—like my grandmother—to grow in a new direction, even after a lifetime of patterns.

"I made it through the darkest part of the night
And now I see the sunrise
Now I feel glorious, glorious."[25]

—MACKLEMORE, "GLORIOUS"

You've been set free. You're no longer chained to the past. You can go anywhere you want to go, and it's time to create your new story.

STRUGGLE IS INEVITABLE

Rich Tedeschi jokes that the best way to explain Buddhism in modern terms is to use an expression popular in military circles: "Embrace the Suck." Buddhism teaches that you must welcome the fact that life is suffering and decide what you want to do about that. Living with this assumption ensures that times of struggle won't destroy your world—even if they shake you. As you create your new story, remember that the one constant in everyone's life is struggle. But now you are able to struggle well.

A number of movie scenes depict characters who have just experienced a major tragedy. The characters cry out, "Why, God?" But this mentality sets you up to think like a victim. You dig yourself a rut, believing that you're being punished by some cosmic injustice. One Marine we met corrected this idea. He said, "God doesn't keep a spreadsheet." There's no force in the universe putting pluses and minuses next to your name, based on something you've done or failed to do, or based on whether or not God likes you.

"Life doesn't happen to you; it happens for you."[26]

—TONY ROBBINS, AUTHOR OF *UNLIMITED POWER* AND *AWAKEN THE GIANT WITHIN*

Struggle is inevitable, not personal. The more productive question to ask, therefore, is simply "Why?" In other words, "What can I learn from this struggle?" This perspective puts the power back in your hands to grow, change, and struggle well.

And probably the best way to talk about struggling well is to talk about death.

WE WON'T MAKE IT OUT ALIVE

At our retreat, we have people spend time writing their own eulogies. "How will the world remember you when you're gone?" we ask. "What do you want people to say about you?" Once each participant has written his or her eulogy, the obvious next question is, "Are you living your life now in a way that ensures that this is how people will describe you when you are gone?"

No one wants to imagine their tombstone reading, "This guy was an asshole"—although some people's choices warrant exactly that. If you want people to remember that you lived a positive, meaningful life, then it's necessary to bring your thoughts, feelings, and actions into congruence. You want to look in the mirror every morning and say, "I have a great deal to offer the world. I am going to give everything I have today and positively impact everyone I encounter."

Your life has a time-horizon. Remembering this *end date* should give you a sense of urgency to live well; it should stoke the desire to be productive, to live a meaningful existence, and to pursue fulfillment—ideally, sooner rather than later. It should also sharpen your perspective about where you're directing your energy. Each choice you make sends you down particular paths that have time limitations. You know you're going to die. So ask the question, "How do I live?"

KEN'S STORY: LOOKING DEATH IN THE FACE

Everyone hits a moment when they have to face their own mortality—and looking death in the face changes you. For me, it was when I broke my back in a parachute jump. I realized that at any given moment, things can change completely. For my wife, it was probably in 2016 when an appendicitis surgery went badly. For seventeen days she was in the hospital—at least two of those days were bad enough that we didn't think she was going to make it. Ultimately, she did recover and is now stronger than before, but the experience was a real wake-up call for both of us. It refocused our priorities and gave us a new sense of urgency to spend our time doing what truly matters.

My dad worked a ton throughout his life. His philosophy was, "Great job, great mattress," and sure enough, he worked hard, then came home and slept well. We had great times with him when he wasn't working, but that wasn't often. One day in his later years, he had a massive heart attack while running on a treadmill in a doctor's office. He needed a quadruple bypass, and afterwards he said, "That's it. It's time for me to change my lifestyle."

He gave his company to my brother and retired. Then, everything changed. He and my stepmom started traveling, working on his homes, and boating. I talked to my dad at least once a day and often twice. His priorities totally shifted. That's what struggle does—it gives you the opportunity to look deeply inside and see what's important.

I had to face death when I was twenty-seven years old; my wife was fifty-eight; my dad was fifty. It happens for all of us at different times, but eventually, we all face death. Many young people literally feel indestructible until something happens that forces them to face death. Maybe it happens when you're a first responder at the site of a mass shooting, or your child is hospitalized, or you're confronted with cancer.

Thinking about your eulogy should get you to consider what truly matters, such as your character. David Brooks, political commentator and columnist for the *New York Times*, talks about this in his book *The Road to Character*—a book he says he wrote "to save his soul."[27] Even after building an enormously successful career, Brooks was personally very unhappy. It was by refocusing his life on character-based priorities that he was able to climb out of his pit.

Life is fragile. The earlier you know that and start living with that reality, the sooner you can live in a way that reflects how you want to be remembered. Then it's a matter of building and living your new story to make it a reality.

REMEMBER THE ALAMO

February 1836, Texas. About 150 rebels stood guard at the Alamo, a citadel of freedom. In the distance, they could see the approach of 2,000 Mexican troops led by the brutal general Santa Anna, with more reinforcements pouring in. These 150 people were a ragtag group of tinkerers, tailors, and gardeners; the professional military experience among them was minimal. Even their leader, Lieutenant Colonel William Travis, was not a Soldier, but a lawyer. Travis's knowledge of military doctrine was limited, but he was relatively sure of one fact: in a siege, things usually don't end well.

Travis considered that the fate of the people in his company would come down to three choices. The first: they could try to run away and escape—the outcome of which would likely be capture, torture, and death. The second: surrender and trust that Santa Anna would allow them to be prisoners of war. However, Travis knew Santa Anna was not the least bit merciful, meaning the likely outcome for the second choice would also be capture, torture, and death. The third option: fight to the end. Only this third choice enabled Travis and his band of brothers to decide how the rest of their lives would transpire. Travis decided that, for him, it had to be Option Three.

He gathered his motley crew and drew a line in the sand in front of him, explaining their three options. "You're welcome to try to escape," he said. Three chose that option, at least one of whom survived—a Frenchman who made it to Louisiana and lived for several more decades. "You can surrender," Travis offered. No one chose the second option. "Or," Travis said, "You can cross this line and choose the nature of the rest of your lives." The remaining 147 people crossed that line, including a Colonel named Jim Bowie who was so badly injured he had to be carried across the line on a cot. Collectively, they decided that the nature of the rest of their lives would be determined by them alone.

"If this call [for aid] is neglected, I am determined to sustain myself as long as possible & die like a soldier who never forgets what is due to his own honor & that of his country—Victory or Death."[28]

—LT. COL. COMDT. WILLIAM BARRETT TRAVIS, IN A
LETTER WRITTEN DURING THE SIEGE OF THE ALAMO

Travis and his 147 Soldiers fought valiantly for thirteen days before Santa Anna's army finally defeated them. Against a trained army of thousands, they lasted for nearly two weeks.

We don't continue to talk about the story of the Alamo because Travis's band was victorious; they knew their deaths were assured before they even began to fight. We remember them because it's the story of people who chose the nature of the rest of their lives. They didn't give up and they didn't give in. Despite the nightmare they faced, they chose the hardest of options—to fight to live and thrive until the end.

In many respects, Travis's stance at the Alamo represents life. You're not going to make it out alive—so, you have a choice to make. Do you run away from your circumstances and hide? Do you give up entirely and accept defeat?

Or, do you fight to the death? Do you give life everything you possibly have, making every remaining moment count? Do you choose courage, seeking to create a life that you can be proud of, whenever your time is called?

The only way to truly live is to walk across that line. Yes, it's scary. Up to this point, the known world may have contained struggle and pain, but it is still a world of certainty. Living as a victim is reassuring if only because of its predictability. At least you know what occurs in that world, knowledge that gives you the illusion of safety and the feeling of comfort. It might feel far easier to let life be chosen for you. However, doing this sentences you to a miserable, inauthentic life.

Across the line, lies the unknown. In order to move forward, you must have a great deal of courage. You must have a great deal of support, and a great deal of practice to be willing to make that journey. But that's where freedom lies. You've got to fight to live.

"When you walk to the edge of all the light you have
and take that first step into the darkness of the unknown,
you must believe that one of two things will happen:
there will be something solid for you to stand upon, or you
will be taught how to fly."[29]

—PATRICK OVERTON, "FAITH"

JOSH'S STORY: TAUGHT TO FLY

I was terrified to step over "Travis's line." The mask I had been wearing for years had resulted in plenty of external validation that looked like success. I had the respect of people who mattered, I had money, I had possessions. And here I was, thinking about walking away from it all.

To let go of that life didn't feel like just letting go of "things;" it required letting go of everything that brought me value. I had to accept that taking this leap would mean surviving without any value in the darkness, for some period of time.

But not making a change was a worse fate. I wasn't living, I was only surviving—and barely, at that.

What was I letting go of, besides an old identity that didn't allow me to live fully, that kept me up at night, made me miserable, and prevented me from enjoying the good things and creating deep relationships? If I kept living that way, I was going to die. Either I would experience a living death by continuing to exist like a zombie, or I would actually end up killing myself. I knew I was losing everything—but to some extent, there was nothing to lose.

I held fast to a quote from Joseph Campbell at the time, which said, "As you go the way of life you will see a great chasm. Jump. It's never as wide as you think."[30] I told myself that the fear I had was far greater than what the situation justified. I had to believe that I was capable of whatever it was that I needed to do. That notion was largely what enabled me to leave on my trip around the world and walk away from the life I'd known.

When I finally got back from my travels, I went to see my old boss, Mort. I told him, "Mort, you saved my life."

"What do you mean?" he asked.

I said, "You gave me *Man's Search for Meaning*. You accepted me where I was. You gave me faith and hope—you saved my life."

He told me, "You know, when you left my house to take that trip, I felt like you were going paragliding. I imagined you running off the side of a cliff. I think most people who do that crash at the bottom and die." He said, "It sounds like you flew."

His words brought tears to my eyes. I said, "Mort, do you know the last thing I did when I took my trip around the world? I went to the Andes in Argentina. I ran off the side of a mountain and I went paragliding. I was up in the air for eighteen minutes." The jump off the cliff *did* enable me to fly.

Years later, I can honestly say I've never been more excited to be alive. It would be hard to argue that getting here wasn't worth moments of profound fear, panic attacks, or even being suicidal. It was all worth it. I had to literally leap off the side of the chasm and hope for the best.

Death happens eventually. It's worth taking the leap into the unknown with faith that good things can happen. On the other side of struggle lies a regained faith in yourself, a faith in the people around you, and the faith that in some way, shape, or form, there's some reason you're still here. There is firm ground to stand on. You might even learn to fly.

CREATING A NEW STORY

Step across the line. Take the leap. Begin a new story. This is inspiring to read—and hard to put into practice.

Why don't people take the risk when the costs of not making a change are so high? There are two main reasons we've encountered. First, people are unconscious of what holds them back. Most people don't even realize that they're acting out patterns of behavior that reflect the training they've experienced. People simply say, "That's how I am." Normally, some kind of a quake is needed before you're able to realize this is not how it's *supposed* to be—it's not how it *has* to be. That "quake" is the gift that emerges from deep struggle. It forces you to examine your life in ways you've never had to before.

Once you understand how you were trained to be, you can decide who and how you want to be. Take a clear look at your patterns and your reactions. If you're aware of them, you can change them. This is why we devote time and energy to helping people build up their understanding of their past experiences and training.

The second inhibitor, as Josh's story illustrates, is fear. It's easier to continue repeating habits and patterns—even if they're not working—than it is to open yourself to the possibility of doing something completely different. For people in this spot, consider: what do you have to lose? What are the costs of not making a change?

We've given you practices to build understanding, and we've supplied many reasons to face the fear of disclosing your story and make a change. At this point, your only way forward is to consciously choose to do the work necessary to begin again.

Make peace with your past, and recognize that it's no longer *your* story, it's just *a* story. You have the opportunity and the responsibility—both to yourself and others—to live a life that authentically reflects who you are and what drives you. When you consciously recognize the sources of your struggle, along with the gifts you possess because of those same experiences, you get the chance to wipe the slate clean. Moving forward is an endeavor that should be hopeful and exhilarating.

Deep struggle gives you this chance to clear the deck. Start working on a new, strong, powerful foundation. You get to determine what that's going to look like; you get the chance to start living life, perhaps for the first time. The rest of this chapter provides you with practices to define who you're seeking to become and how you're going to get there.

REFLECT ON WHO YOU ARE

One of the gifts the military gives Soldiers is a code: behavioral expectations are crystal clear. Everyone knows exactly what's implied if someone declares, "That's not how a Marine behaves." There's a clear guide that directs decisions and actions. We don't have that moral clarity in our society, which leads to plenty of confusion.

We want to help you form your own code, one that defines who you want to be in the world, and what you want to do. Your code becomes a compass to help you navigate new opportunities and times of struggle. However, this code can't come from a place outside of you—there's no sergeant waiting around the corner with clear directions about how to live and barking orders to go with it. This code needs to come from within you—it needs to be yours.

Why? Many of our readers have lived too long as a peripheral character in their own stories. You've either played the victim, or you've played the villain, taking your aggression out on other sympathetic characters. Either you've had things done to you, or you're doing bad things to other people. This is no way to live. There's no freewill in this kind of life; there's no joy.

In our program, we talk about warriors being those who protect and serve other people, who refuse to be a victim of circumstance, and who never use past experiences as an excuse for bad decision-making. Warriors, in other words, choose to be the main characters in their own stories. They're not victims; they're not villains. They're the good guys—the ones you root for.

Just as a screenwriter sits down to write a movie script, you have some key questions to ask as you think about the kind of protagonist you want to be. What kind of person is the main character? What is he or she about? What is meaningful to her? What matters to him? What are the main character's priorities and principles?

Maybe it's easy to start by thinking of yourself in the third person, but eventually, the questions need to get personal. We recommend that people start by exploring three key inquiries, each of which is connected to a fundamentally important aspect of living:

- Identity: Who am I?
- Sense of purpose: Why am I here?
- Connection: Where do I belong?

By the end of this chapter, you should be on your way to answering some of these crucial questions. As you continue to put yourself out into the world, your answers to these questions may evolve. You might go to Christian churches, Buddhist temples, Jewish gatherings, foreign countries, twelve-step groups, new classes—the new places you explore and the new people you encounter will all play a role in helping you develop your answers to the three questions above.

Hopefully that journey lasts for the rest of your life. As Josh's grandmother said, "You're always evolving, shaping, and changing." Struggle may feel brutal to endure, but it forces the opportunity to figure out who you are.

You want to become the movie protagonist others recognize as being authentic in the midst of struggle. Exploring the answers to these questions helps build up your genuine understanding of who you are. Maybe you don't always act like the hero, but it's obvious that you're doing your best to live honestly, to live truly, to take action into your own hands for the betterment of others.

Both of us have crafted hard copy answers to these types of questions, and we return to them regularly. After Josh returned from his trip around the world, he sat down on his couch and wrote out twenty guiding principles to live by. Ken does goal exercises and completes his own assessments and reflections. We both believe that you've got to clearly see what you're shooting at, in order to know if you're hitting the target. Further into this chapter, we've created prompts to help you begin drafting your own "code."

OPPORTUNITY COMES FROM DEEP STRUGGLE

Continue thinking about yourself as a screenwriter for a moment. Often in movies, the protagonist is prepared for his or her unique challenge by earlier trials. The same is true in real life; your individual struggles have prepared you for your individual purpose.

At first glance, suffering seems senseless. One veteran we worked with is burned on 95 percent of his body. He's missing both of his arms, and his head's disfigured from the burns. Struggles like these would be senseless—and surely *are* senseless—if you don't hang on to one critical belief. Suffering exists for one reason: to serve as a wake-up call. Struggle forces you to realize that the path you're on isn't the path you should be on.

Opportunities for transformation are almost entirely rooted in deep struggle or suffering, because they force you to change. Like in the story of the Alamo, you don't have a choice to go back to the way things were. You either have to live or die. Struggle presents you with a stark choice. If you have a Stage Four cancer diagnosis and are told you have three months to live, what do you do with that?

Some struggles are undeniably more extreme than others. The Holocaust and the Hanoi Hilton are examples of suffering on the far end of the spectrum. Perhaps we could point to these experiences as the height of injustice, and rightly so—but it's also a reminder that people who have endured the worst suffering can thrive the most because of their experiences. Even at the height of suffering, there is the knowledge that the worst of stories can lead to success and hope.

We also want to clarify that smaller struggles may be equally as significant in impacting a person's life. Every individual is able to deal with a different level of struggle—and that's okay.

JOSH'S STORY: PURPOSE FOUND FROM A SMALLER STORM

I did an interview with a Marine on All Marine Radio, and after telling him my story, he scoffed. He said, "I don't mean to be rude, Josh, but you sound like a total wuss."

I said, "Well, Mac, by your standards, that's true. But I don't have your strength, training, or experiences. I wasn't raised to be tough." My tolerance for struggle was much lower than his. As a result, I had the capacity to weather a smaller storm than some of the people I work with. The size of the storm is relative though—the events I went through still changed my life.

My story may not be that dramatic. I wasn't in a terrorist incident, and I didn't lose everything in a natural disaster;

my struggle came out of pretty routine circumstances. But that's the point—the fact that people can achieve growth in the worst of times is a reminder that anything short of that still can provide fuel for change.

What's more, the nature of my struggle helped spotlight my future calling. When I was struggling, there were a couple people who kept me alive, but I largely didn't have the support that I needed. I also didn't have a notion that it was possible for me to build a fulfilling life. Those deficits in the midst of my struggle have made me passionate about bringing that support and hope to other people now. I want to make sure the practices for struggling well are available to others; I know how useful they are, because I didn't have them.

The ideas about who we want to become and what we're meant to be doing might seem like distant truths—something we could only discover in an old book that we don't even know how to find. But the truth is, those answers can be found much closer to home. Your calling often relates to something that benefited you when you desperately needed help, or something you didn't have, yet learned the value of—as in my case.

KEN'S STORY: STRENGTH AND CALLING

We're all made up differently, and we have different levels

of strength. Normally, the trauma and the training that you have as you're growing up is what creates your ability to handle adversity. Those areas where you're especially strong can end up leading you to opportunities where you're uniquely qualified to serve.

In my life, for example, I spent a lot of time beside my mom's hospital bed when I was a kid. She was in and out of the hospital on heavy doses of chemotherapy; then she was in a coma. For probably two years, we spent time with my mom in the hospital, holding her hand. I can still remember the chunks of hair that came out when my grandmother brushed it.

I think it's likely that my experience with my mom helped me develop the strength required to sit by severely wounded guys' hospital beds. I took my oldest daughter up to the hospital once, and we visited an amputee. He had his leg up in the air and was showing us where the surgery had just occurred. There wasn't any blood, but it was a fresh stitch job over a large wound. The sight was too much for my daughter—she needed to be taken out of the room by the nurses. But that stuff never affected me. Not that I'm a big strong guy, but I'd been to the hospital over and over and over again. I had been trained to be strong in this area.

Those hospital visits ended up leading me to my calling. I

was able to sit by these guys' beds and listen to the horrific stories. I talked to guys who had lost their eyes and saw blood coming from their eye sockets. Ultimately, it was through listening to these stories that I realized amputees and severely wounded warriors tended to possess an amazing strength. Questioning why that might be, led me into this work with Posttraumatic Growth.

A LIFE OF SERVICE

It may be clear in both of our stories that the most fulfilling and successful work we've done has been in a service capacity. That's no coincidence. Both of us have experienced the emptiness in pursuing the widely accepted definition of American success: we've pounded the pavement to make money, with little personal fulfillment.

Although many people define success in terms of material possessions, for us, that doesn't cut it. And for most people in fact, material possessions are a facade.

Research studies show there's no increase in happiness between people who make an income of $75,000 and people who make up to $2 million.[31] Once people get beyond meeting their needs, they get into "wants;" ironically, the "wants" can drag you down. Pursuing "wants" puts you on a hedonistic treadmill. You used to want a Honda, now you want an Audi, then you want a Mercedes, then you want a Ferrari. Yet satisfaction from any material item tends to be fleeting—and this is coming from two guys who love sports cars.

Furthermore, wealthier societies, like the United States, aren't happier than poorer nations. In 2016, the US recorded a thirty-year suicide high rate, even though we're the wealthiest country in the world.[32] A Gallup survey called, "The State of the American Workplace," says that 33 percent of US employees are engaged at work.[33] Only a third of the country reports even being *engaged* in the work they do. This means that nearly 70 percent of Americans hate their jobs! If you remember Ken's dad's mantra about the two keys to life (a good job and a good mattress), it is no wonder that so many people are struggling.

We believe the absence of meaning is largely what plunges people into the React Sine Wave pattern of life. Take our military personnel for instance. In the military, they have a belief system, a service-oriented environment, and are given purpose and community. When dropped back into a largely self-serving culture, and taking a job that doesn't engage them—these men and women can easily run into personal crises and times of profound struggle.

So what is worth pursuing? Where does lasting joy come from? What creates that intangible sense of pleasure that remains—the stuff of significance?

Let's go back to the Wellness Triangle. We strongly believe that each of the three outer categories are important to living a "successful" life. Without strong mental, physical, and financial wellness, you're going to have a tough time.

However, it's the center of that triangle that's most critical. Stories of natural disasters in developing countries make this obvious. Many people in Haiti suffered huge blows after the earthquake in 2012; financially, they were ruined. Mentally, they suffered extreme distress. Physically, they faced hunger, thirst, and illness. But many Haitians are strong people of faith, and that spiritual center sustained them. There was a hope that something better would come along. One pastor preached this message to his congregation: "If you are still alive, it is because you have something to do on this Earth, now."[34] There was faith that their tragedy could be redeemed, and their spiritual beliefs gave them strength to endure and rebuild.

In times of struggle, your strongest sustaining power does not come from financial security, intelligence, or physical strength. It comes from the center of your triangle. We don't define spirituality in religious terms, although we recognize that religious faith can be helpful. Mainly, we define healthy spirituality in terms of one's character, relationships, and service to others. Even when other areas of life fall apart—you've had a brain injury, you're in debt, you're physically injured—still, by doing things for others, you can shore up your whole system.

For that reason, our definition of success is simple. Successful living is: doing better today than you did yesterday. "Doing better" looks different for everyone, based on the goals people individually define for themselves, referencing the areas of their Wellness Triangle. The goals related to the outside of the triangle help you accomplish meaningful goals in strengthening your own life. The goals related to the center of the triangle help you develop purpose, fulfillment, and meaning as you seek to serve and strengthen the lives of others.

"No individual has any right to come into the world, and go out of it without leaving behind him a distinct and legitimate reason for having passed through it."[35]

—GEORGE WASHINGTON CARVER

You have a responsibility to provide a reason for why you lived. The military contains people who are born and trained to serve—but in actuality, that's in all of us. We all are born to serve. It's through serving others that you'll achieve the meaningful life you crave, and create a story worth living.

PRACTICAL STEPS: SELF-REFLECTION

Let's get practical. This next section takes you through a process of reflection that helps you consider your principles and beliefs. You'll think in big picture terms about the kind of person you want to be. From there, we'll help you identify specific goals in each of your Wellness Triangle categories that practically help you become that person. Our last section gets into concrete action steps to enable you to accomplish those goals.

WHO YOU WERE

You've now spent the last days, weeks, or months reading this book; we've asked you to reflect and write as you walk this journey with us. At this point, we'd like you to take a moment and look back where you started.

In Chapter Two, you recorded scores in each of your Wellness Triangle categories that reflected where you were when you began reading this book. Re-record those scores here:

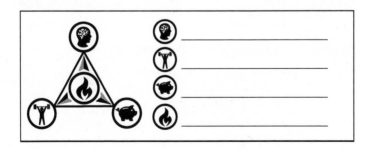

WHO ARE YOU?

It's possible that the scores you wrote down in Chapter Two no longer reflect where you are. After reading this book, going over the experiences you've had, the gifts you possess, the challenges you've already navigated, and making peace with your past, it's likely you're already in a different place. Particularly if you've begun to incorporate wellness practices in your life more regularly, there may already be a noticeable shift. You may feel more grounded, more prepared for the future, and you may recognize more of a connection between your head and your heart. Perhaps, more simply, you're finally telling yourself the truth.

So, for the second time, we're asking you to rate your Wellness Triangle, on a scale of one to five in each area: mind, body, finances, and spirit. Where are you? If five is near perfection, and one is barely getting by, where are you in the area of mind, in terms of focus, motivation, and creativity? Where are you in body, in terms of strength, sleep, and nutrition? Where are you financially, in terms of savings, employment, and your quality of life? And where are you spiritually in terms of your character, relationships, and your service to others?

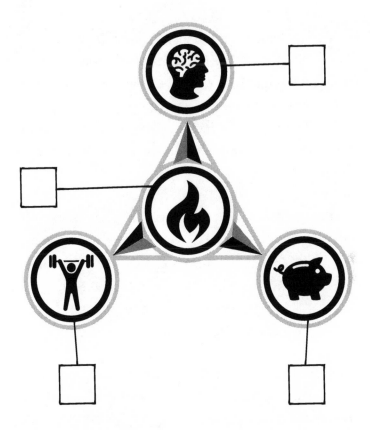

Now you've had the chance to look back on your past and reflect on how this new information has affected you. We want you to take a deep look at who you are right now. It's time to ask yourself the three existential questions we hit on earlier.

Key Questions to Ask

When the connection between your head and heart is restored, and your Wellness Triangle is strong, you can make conscious choices about who you want to become. These choices should be determined not by other people, or cultural pressures, but on three conclusions generated by you. These conclusions should arrive as the answers to the three big-picture inquiries we identified earlier in the chapter. With each, we've provided specific questions to help you develop your responses.

1. *Identity: Who am I?*
   A. Principles: What is it I hold most dear? What are the 3-5 principles that I want to guide my decision-making, no matter how I feel or what I think?
   B. Character: What are my strengths, and what am I capable of? What are my gifts?

2. *Sense of purpose: Why am I here?*
   A. Passions: What do I care most deeply about? Why do I feel passionate about these particular things?
   B. Beliefs: What do I believe about the world? What do I think is possible? What have I learned from my struggle that I want to share with others?

3. *Connection: Where do I belong? Who will I serve?*
   A. Connection to Self: What practices in my life help me struggle well and live well?
   B. Connection to Others: Who am I with when I feel the most joy? Who are my 3-5 closest acquaintances? Who do I feel drawn to support and serve?

WHO ARE YOU SEEKING TO BECOME?

Imagine yourself twelve months from now. It's been nearly a year since you picked up a copy of *Struggle Well* and read it. In the past year, you've established yourself as a person that people respect and look up to, someone admired by their friends and loved by their family. You're filled with purpose, balance, and you know where you are going. You are well and working hard in mind, body, finance, and spirit. Others describe you as a deeply principled person, a person of character.

Imagine going through the paces of a typical morning inside this new self—waking up, getting dressed, drinking coffee, walking out to your car. Feel what it means to walk through the world at peace with yourself and with others. Taste what it's like, knowing that each moment is precious and something to savor. Smell the success and the fruits of all your hard work. Hear the sounds of the world you encounter, the birds, the breeze, and the activity of life. See the joy on the faces of those around you and the way they light up in your presence.

Each day you wake up motivated, focused, connected, and congruent. You are grateful for the blessing of a new day and all the possibilities it brings. You look in the mirror each morning knowing who you are and exactly what to do.

Now, from the deepest part of your heart and your spirit, consider: "Who are you?" In big-picture terms, how would you describe yourself twelve months from now? Perhaps you would define yourself in terms of, "I am a student," "I am balanced," "I am a loving father." It might also be helpful to think of how others would describe you in a year: "...a hard-working teacher who enjoys her work and loves her family."

Then, think about who your future self is, in terms of the Wellness Triangle. Begin with your mind. Having a strong mind means you're motivated, focused, learning new things, and challenging yourself. So, twelve months from now, what kind of person are you in terms of your mind? Are you reading books? Are you taking classes? Have you been having deep conversations with people in your support network? Are you meditating? What do your specific mental Wellness Practices look like?

What kind of person are you physically in twelve months? How have you been taking care of your body? Are you eating well? How often are you exercising? How are you sleeping? What does it feel like to move through your day in a stronger, more energetic, and flexible body?

In one year, what kind of person are you financially? What debts have been chipped away at, or eliminated? How have you educated yourself about personal finance in the past twelve months? How have you added to your long-term savings and retirement accounts? What does it feel like to go to the ATM these days, and see the numbers in your checking and savings accounts? What kind of work are you doing?

Where are you spiritually, one year from now? Who are the people you're most deliberately investing in? How have your patterns of interaction with those people changed, as you've tried to be less selfish and serve those loved ones? What new people have you encountered, doing service projects in your community? How have your eyes opened to the world around you, as you've raised your gaze past your own challenges?

Take a moment to consider these questions and formulate your answers in the table provided. Under each category, complete the sentence, "I am..." For example, we once worked with a farmer named Jeff who developed the following answers to the "I am" statements:

Who am I: "I'm a humble farmer who can take care of my family and the people I care about."

Mental Wellness: "I am clear headed, I am motivated, I am focused, and I am able to complete the tasks I set forth."

Physical Wellness: "I'm strong and able to complete tasks around the farm without injury."

Financial Wellness: "I run a self-sustaining farming operation that allows me to save for retirement and the things we enjoy doing."

Spiritual Wellness: "I am connected to a higher power and to those I love, including my girlfriend and my animals."

In a moment, we'll have you consider the specific actions you might take to accomplish these "I am" statements, but initially, just focus on the different aspects of who you desire to become a year from now.

I AM _____

_____

_____

I AM _____ _____ _____ _____ _____	I AM _____ _____ _____ _____ _____
I AM _____ _____ _____ _____ _____	I AM _____ _____ _____ _____ _____

GOAL SETTING: THE "HOW" OF YOUR NEW STORY

Now, it's necessary to consider specific actions related to each of these statements. This is part of working toward a congruent life; you've identified the kind of person you aspire to be, which relates to your thoughts and feelings. Next, you need to identify the actions that accompany your thoughts and feelings.

Remember: you are what you repeatedly do. Your actions are the clearest reflection of who you are in the world, and it's your choice to take action that ultimately changes your life. This next section walks you through the process of developing SMART goals (specific, measurable, achievable, realistic, and time-specific) to get you from Point A to Point B.

"When you know how you want to spend the rest of your life, you want the rest of your life to start as soon as possible."[36]
—PARAPHRASED FROM THE MOVIE,
WHEN HARRY MET SALLY

You might feel like cracking the whip on this process—you want the rest of your life to start immediately! But you don't get from Point A to Point B via teleportation; there's no genie who instantly produces this transformation in you. The critical aspects of accomplishing goals are hard work and patience. We're going to guide you toward a slow and steady approach that you can consistently stick to.

We've talked about the dangers of shortcutting the transformative process; remember Dusty with the tree-trunk arms, who told Josh that he needed to "unfuck himself" before helping anyone else? Although we might want to bypass the hard work of changing ourselves internally, this is a process of dedication and commitment, of intentionality, and diligence. Change requires hard work.

"The journey of a thousand miles starts with a single step."[37]

—LAU TZU

The journey is a massive part of the entire experience. You want to get "there," but the countless steps you take to achieve your goals are part of what ultimately transforms you into the person you want to become. The "ups and the downs" that go along with this journey help mold your character in new ways. You want to start to map where you're going so you have a clear idea of how you're going to get there. Remember to bring patience along with your principles as you do; this is not a quick process.

People who are successful in the military, in business, in government, and every other walk of life have one key practice in common: they set goals, hold themselves accountable, complete goals, and set new goals. They develop a clear mission and sense of direction, which enables them to be successful. They also commit to hard work, dedication, and making conscious choices.

It's one thing to write goals down, which a lot of people do. It's another thing to have the determination and the discipline to complete them. We're going to do everything we can in written form to give you the necessary aid to do this. We'll walk you through the healthy process of goal setting, ensuring you set them up and write them properly, and we'll talk about how to find an accountability partner to hold you to your goals.

GOAL-SETTING

The first step in goal-setting is to clearly define what you want to accomplish and publicly communicate that to a person you trust: "I want to accomplish this, in these four areas: mind, body, finances, and spirit." Later in this section, we'll talk about the characteristics of an accountability partner who is the ideal person to share that information with.

The second step is reverse-engineering the series of steps required to complete the goal. Perhaps, in your Physical Wellness section of the "I am" table, you wrote, "I am healthy, I am more energetic, and I am strong." This is a big-picture answer, and as such, it's theoretical and abstract. You need to translate your answer(s) into actionable goal steps. If you're currently in the habit of eating unhealthy food and living a sedentary lifestyle, then you've identified a starting place: Point A. The end goal is that clear articulation of your mission: "I'm going to lose twenty pounds." That's your Point B.

From Point B, you work backward in a process called "goal factoring." Essentially, you identify a series of steps, broken into thirty-day stretches, which connect back to

Point A. You first set the vision ("I am healthy"), and then set the mission ("I will lose twenty pounds"), and then set incremental goals to accomplish the mission.

Perhaps you do the math and determine that the only way to accomplish your goal of losing twenty pounds is to exercise three days a week and reduce your daily intake by one thousand calories. However—before you get there, you need to be consistent about getting to the gym three days a week and reducing your intake by five hundred calories. And before you get there, you need to consistently get to the gym at least once a week, and stop drinking soda. Before you get there, you need to get a gym membership, and to consult a nutritionist.

Each incremental step should be based on thirty-day stretches, working backward from your end goal to your starting point. You would compose these step-by-step goals for each different section of your Wellness Triangle, using this process of reverse engineering.

SMART GOALS

The critical aspect of setting goals well, is to be SMART: specific, measurable, achievable, realistic, and time-specific. If you set goals that aren't achievable, you'll destroy your confidence and momentum before you even start. Setting SMART goals prevents you from overdoing it, which can easily lead to burnout and failure. But the slow-and-steady approach that SMART goals establish means that you're more likely to over-perform your goals, than fail at achieving them—that's a good problem.

Let's continue using weight loss as an illustration. People often set bad weight loss goals: "I want to lose ten pounds by the end of the week so I look good at my high school reunion." A goal stated like this fails some of the key SMART requirements. Attempting to lose ten pounds in a week is certainly not possible using any kind of healthy or sustainable diet methods; it's largely unachievable and not realistic. There's also no plan stated for how this unrealistic goal would even be accomplished.

A SMART goal corrects these issues. Maybe after doing some research, you determine that it's healthy for someone with your current weight to lose one pound a week. Your SMART goal might be, "I'm going to lose ten pounds in ten weeks by exercising four times a week and reducing my daily calorie intake by five hundred calories." This goal meets the SMART criteria: it is specific by identifying ten pounds. It's measurable because you'll be able to track your weight, your time at the gym, and your calorie intake. It's achievable because it is scientifically within the realm of possibility. It's realistic because there's a supporting plan to get into the gym and reduce your calorie count. It is also time-oriented because you've identified a duration of ten weeks.

SMART goals are not hard to carry out: go to the gym three times a week; meditate twice a day; pay X amount of debt down; do one good thing for somebody else once a month; have a weekly date night with your spouse. These goals should be easy to accomplish and ladder up into life-changing accomplishments that are truly meaningful. You'll know you've developed a good set of goals if you look at your list and think, "That looks simple enough."

"Opportunity is missed by most people because it is dressed in overalls and looks like work."[38]

—THOMAS EDISON

SMART goals are simple and easy—but they still require hard work to accomplish. You have to create the conditions for success in your life by taking intentional action. That means you need to be purposeful about your choices, your time management, and your strategy in driving toward the life you want. It's not enough to merely decide you want to be a different person; if you don't take intentional action required to be a different person, you're not going to get there.

The gym is always full in January with well-intentioned people who earnestly desire to be more fit. By March, the gym is empty. Good intentions are not enough. SMART goals better equip you to make progress one step at a time, but they won't become anything more than words on a page without your intentionality and accountability.

We believe that you have a 95 percent likelihood of accomplishing your goals if you adhere to a particular goal-driven process. First, set a smart goal that's legitimately SMART. Second: reflect on the resources you need. Third: think about the challenges that might prevent you from being successful and form solutions to those. Fourth: create action steps. And fifth: engage with someone at least monthly to provide support and hold you accountable.

Yes, there's a small chance that circumstances beyond your control may impede you from getting there—but if all the other pieces are in place, that margin of error is miniscule. If you can stack up success at a 95 percent rate, twelve times in a year, you'll accomplish massive progress in every facet of your life.

ACCOUNTABILITY PARTNERS AND SUBJECT MATTER EXPERTS

"Quitting cold turkey." The phrase conjures up images of people who were able to cease a bad habit instantly, easily, and permanently. For most people though, the process of changing patterns is not so easily done; you'll be far more successful with support and accountability in pursuing goals.

There are generally two accountability needs for people looking to successfully carry out these goals. The first is an accountability partner, which we recommend you find in your three-to-five support network. You need somebody you trust to check in on you and help motivate you. A partner might call you up weekly. "Hey man, just checking in. You said you were going to lose a pound this week. What did you start at? What did you lose or gain?"

The accountability partner doesn't need to have any real expertise in the area of your goal; he or she simply needs to provide the consistent support you need to get there. They'll provide this accountability not in a way that shames you, but in a way that respects your desire to improve in your four wellness areas and helps spur you on. If you know that weekly call is coming, you'll be more motivated to get out of bed in the early morning and get yourself to the gym.

In some cases though, you may need the knowledge of a subject matter expert to get the ball rolling. For instance, if you haven't been to the gym in fifteen years and have a bad knee, it might be important to start pursuing your goal with the help of an expert, like a fitness coach or a personal trainer. If you've been eating fast food on a daily basis, and need nutritional advice on how to change your diet, you might need the expertise of a nutritionist. These subject matter experts can provide knowledge and resources to help you formulate the most realistic, productive plan for achieving your goals.

Once knowledge and resources are established, the baton can be passed back to your accountability partner. You might come away from a meeting with a nutritionist with new recipes to try and a list of foods to clean out of your pantry. Your accountability partner is going to be the person who ensures you toss the candy and chips, and stock your fridge with fruits and vegetables. The accountability partner may also help lead you to the subject matter experts you need.

Accountability partners should also help you track your progress in meeting your goals. Weekly check-ins are ideal, as they allow partners to discuss progress and make changes if necessary. Perhaps you tell your accountability partner, "I know I originally wanted to do this goal in four weeks, but I'm going to need five—because my life just got a little bit complicated." A good accountability partner might acknowledge the challenge of your present circumstances, but also sets a time to check in again soon, and suggests ways you can get yourself back on your original timeline. They'll assist you in tracking the measurable parts of your goal: how many days at the gym, how many servings of vegetables? They'll ask needed questions: "Did you meet with your trainer? Did you try the spin class like you said you were going to?"

These partners shouldn't shame you, but they also shouldn't go easy on you. If you destroy your diet one evening in a binge of beer and ice cream, it's counterproductive for your accountability partner to tell you you're a failure. However, it's equally counterproductive for him or her to say, "No worries—you deserve a night off! Diets never work anyway." Good accountability partners tell you the hard truth if necessary, and help you get back on track. They'll brainstorm with you about ways to correct your actions when necessary and remind you why you're pursuing your goals in the first place.

In basic training, Marines nurture the idea of an internal locus of control; the idea is that our actions influence our external environment, as opposed to what we typically think—the external environment influences us. As Marines set out to complete The Crucible, a forty-eight-mile hike involving food and sleep deprivation, they're encouraged to propel each other on, using this internal locus of control. If somebody is struggling, a fellow Marine looks at that person and says, "Why are you doing this? Why is this important?" The struggling Marine responds with his internal motivation—his why: "I'm doing this to create a better life for my family. I'm doing this for my daughter. I'm doing this for my wife. I'm doing this for me."

Once you identify why something matters, you'll get it done. A good accountability partner helps you remember why that goal is important to you and won't let you make excuses. You want people who say, "Hey, you said you were going to be in the gym every day for the next three weeks, and you're not here. Your ass better be here tomorrow." You need people who push you with the hard truth when necessary. If your accountability partner is in your three-to-five network, then it's likely there's a shared trust there; this trust ensures your partner remains honest with you, and that you'll listen and respond to what he or she says.

Now that we've discussed how to create your goals and who to create them with, it's time to get something written down. We've supplied a table for you to identify goals in each Wellness Category, over the next thirty days. You will start by setting five goals: one in each of the outer Wellness Triangle categories of mind, body, and finances, and two goals for spiritual. Make sure that the goals you write down are SMART!

It's likely that you'll want to come up with more than one goal per wellness category, and may want to envision steps that go beyond your first thirty-day stretch. We encourage our readers to take this exercise beyond these pages, and begin completing a document that allows you to be as thorough as you'd like. You can access SMART goal worksheets on our website at strugglewell.com.

SMART Goals: My First 30 Days
Specific, Measurable, Achievable, Realistic, & Time-specific

Mental Wellness SMART Goal: _____
_____

Physical Wellness SMART Goal: _____
_____

Financial Wellness SMART Goal: _____
_____

Spiritual Wellness SMART Goal (Relationships): _____
_____

Spiritual Wellness SMART Goal (Service): _____
_____

At first, goal setting may feel like over-scripting your life. It can feel forced and a bit contrived. However, as you do it and get into a rhythm, the process becomes second nature quickly; that's true with any wellness practice. You're building new, healthy habits.

Best of all, as you set goals, you'll find they start to be self-reinforcing, impacting areas of your life that you never thought possible. For instance, if you have a spiritual wellness goal to enhance your three-to-five network, and a mental wellness goal to start meditating, you may end up meeting grounded, balanced people who become a healthy new presence in your three-to-five network. Goal setting can become increasingly efficient; one goal can end up knocking down all ten pins, as opposed to one at a time.

WHAT'S AT STAKE?

Maybe you picked up our book because you're struggling. Like, really struggling. You bought the book, you've read this far, and you've absorbed a lot of our concepts. Maybe some of it, you've mentally logged away as important; maybe some of it, you've discarded. Maybe you've read through this chapter with the thought, "At some point, I should go back and try to fill these tables out."

Then you put the book down, forget about it, and life continues on. You don't change. Struggle still arrives, and it drags you down every time.

Absorbing information is well and good, but without taking action, you remain stuck. If you continue down your current path, fail to set goals, or don't listen to your accountability partner, you won't experience the kind of meaningful change you're longing for. The road from struggle to strength requires this movement; taking these steps is how you achieve Posttraumatic Growth.

Let us encourage you. We've had the privilege of seeing literally thousands of people take this journey from despair to joy. This process isn't just worth it—it *works*. Taking these steps leads you out of the prison of your mind into a liberating, thriving life.

Doing nothing commits you to the alternative—you remain in the cell. You consign yourself to living the life of other people's expectations and suppress your own needs and desires. We've urged and guided you to discover where you want to go; consider the cost if you don't start walking there.

"Death isn't the greatest loss in life; the greatest loss is what dies inside while still alive."[39]

—TUPAC SHAKUR

You can choose to continually put to death what is inside of you, or bring it to life and allow it to shine. When you make the conscious choice to invest in the person you want to become, you become that person. It's the greatest gift that you can give yourself and to the world.

Remember the Alamo. Remember Travis's line in the sand. Step over the line. Choose for yourself the nature of the rest of your life.

CHAPTER SIX

TO SERVE YOURSELF, YOU MUST SERVE OTHERS

———

"Life's most persistent and urgent question is: what are you doing for others?"[40]

—MARTIN LUTHER KING, JR.

There's a reason it's called Military Service. From the moment a recruit shows up at boot camp, individual identity is hammered at, pounded down, and ultimately taken away. In its place, recruits are taught to focus on others. This creates an incredible community of mutual trust. Soldiers learn that if everyone does their job, everyone gets what they need.

The community of service goes beyond the men and women engaged in combat. For every Soldier on the battlefield, it takes five to ten non-combatants to provide support to that individual in areas like medical aid, food, logistics, and so on. Combatants learn they don't need to look out for themselves, because so many others are already looking out for them. As each Soldier participates in this network of service, his or her life is afforded meaning and purpose.

It's no surprise, therefore, that Soldiers often struggle to reconnect when they come home. The culture they return to prioritizes a focus on self. Civilians are largely taught to be independent, to compete with others for prized spots, to "get theirs." No longer does the Soldier exist within a trusted community, all working together toward a common goal; no longer is there a clear sense of purpose in day-to-day life.

Unless—the Soldier finds new ways to serve.

Finding ways to provide service to a community is profoundly valuable. Not only does it build deeper connections with other people, it also helps counteract isolation and shame, because you become part of something bigger than yourself. Service provides aid to people who need it, which in turn provides a sense of purpose to the person serving. Furthermore, the research on Posttraumatic Growth shows that the most significant growth occurs from helping others.

And yet—our chapter title starts off with, "To serve yourself..." You might be wondering, "Is this section of the book really going to be about living selflessly for the benefit of others? Or is it going to endorse service so I start feeling better?"

Well, both.

Here's what we believe: healthy people help people. Wounded people wound people. If, in fact, you can achieve growth after trauma, the best thing you can do for the world is to provide a helping hand to others on their journey. Tedeschi's work on Posttraumatic Growth describes service to others as the pinnacle of the journey from struggle to strength. However, you can't help others until you are in a healthy place yourself.

This chapter discusses the enormous personal and community benefits that result when we engage in service, and it also defines *healthy* service. If you try to serve in a way that's unsustainable or that compromises your own health, then you're not helping anyone. In those cases, you jeopardize the community you're attempting to serve, and risk damaging yourself. The timing and scale at which you serve other people must be balanced against your own level of personal health.

THE VALUE OF SERVICE

When done right, service is a sustainable, renewable, fulfilling fuel for your spirit. As Josh's story can attest, living life purely for ego and material success does nothing to make you happy. You can have a beautiful outer Wellness Triangle, but with no spiritual center that mask is all you have. Life is a hollow world, driven not by substance, but by how your shell is perceived.

However, when you realize that there's a real need for the talents and skills you possess—not for your own enrichment, but to enrich the world in some meaningful way—you'll experience profound fulfillment and satisfaction. Why?

Service shifts our focus from "naval gazing" to outward gazing. When you struggle, it's easy to indulge in self-pity: "I didn't sleep well, I'm anxious and depressed, I'm lethargic..." Your focus fixates on your own ailments and symptoms. However, the moment you go to a soup kitchen and you're helping people, you forget about yourself. Your perspective is widened as you remember the other people who are struggling as well—many, to a greater extent than you. In those moments, you drop the self-pity and you're able to be present with the people you're serving.

These moments of human connection can help with some of the most debilitating aspects of struggle. Hopelessness comes from feeling disconnected, unworthy, and not valuable. Service enables people to find ways to connect deeply with other human beings. When you're in a line of people packing lunch bags for kids, or helping rescue efforts during an emergency, barriers to connection fall away. Connecting with others helps counter shame, which makes you more readily able to access your heart. The deeper parts of yourself—your values, feelings, and principles—are within reach. This creates the space you need to *respond* in hard situations, rather than react, enabling you to make conscious choices that you'll feel good about.

To better understand this idea of space, imagine a rookie quarterback versus an experienced NFL quarterback—one who's spent years leading his team on the field. If either quarterback is given two seconds behind their offensive line to make a decision and complete a pass, those quarterbacks will feel those two seconds very differently. The two seconds for the rookie quarterback will feel like 0.2 seconds. Rookies always say, "The game's so fast at this level, it's so fast!" But the experienced quarterback can make those two seconds feel like thirty. The experience of his career gives him the space he needs to respond to the events playing out on the field, rather than react.

The difference between reacting and responding is space, which allows you to take a beat before you do something. You create this internal space by connecting your head and your heart, using what we've described: disclosure, wellness practices, a strong three-to-five network...and, not least of all, by serving others. When you create that connection and space, you have the ability to play chess in a world of checkers. You get to be the experienced quarterback who's orchestrating his world with grace, calm, ease, and responsiveness, as opposed to reacting with fear at everything coming at you. If you have space, you can remain in a place where you're making thoughtful, congruent choices.

As Josh's story can also attest though, attempting "spiritual bypass" via service before getting healthy yourself is dangerous. Without doing the hard work of dealing with your past, connecting the head and heart, and learning to self-regulate, some people try to get the "high" of service by jumping right into an intense area of need, hoping to distract themselves from their own struggle. Inevitably, they bring their own struggle into the equation as they try to help other people; their counsel of others is skewed by their own stunted health. Again—wounded people wound people. There's a balance: you have to take care of yourself, *so that* you can take care of others.

START SMALL

We recommend starting with the small stuff. Some areas of service require people with robust spiritual and mental health—areas like mentoring troubled youth, or starting up a nonprofit, or signing up for the Peace Corps. That's the "big stuff," and these are not areas where you should start serving. However, other "smaller" areas of service can accommodate people who are in the midst of their own struggle, providing meaningful ways to experience the benefits of service in a way that doesn't produce spiritual bypass or jeopardize others.

Think of these acts of service as "transactional;" you show up, you provide an act of service, and then you leave with your spirit uplifted, knowing you provided necessary aid. Transactional acts of service might be serving at a soup kitchen, or the humane society, or a food bank. Perhaps you commit to doing small acts of kindness every Sunday, or you participate in a volunteer service project, like Habitat for Humanity or ringing the Salvation Army's bell.

Service efforts like these are hard to mess up. Maybe you serve too much food, or serve too slowly, but the margin of error is limited. The "smallness" of these endeavors doesn't take away from your healing or your family's healing; they also don't jeopardize the community you're trying to serve. However, they do enable you to get started, connect with other like-minded people, and begin discovering areas of giving back that you enjoy.

For some, even recommending that you do the small stuff

sounds daunting. On one side of the spectrum, many people feel the temptation to do nothing and remain passive. You'd rather not put yourself out there; it's easier to just watch another episode on Netflix, even if it means you wake up feeling depressed again the next morning. On the other side of the spectrum are the people who tend to go overboard; they commit to too much, too fast, and inevitably burn out.

Assess your inclination. If your inclination is to be passive, you'll have to push yourself to find these service opportunities. If your inclination is to go overboard, then seek to begin slowly. But try *something*. Stop making excuses in the midst of your struggle, and re-engage with the world. You may not land on an area of service that captures your passions immediately, but the process of discovery is valuable in and of itself. Both of us found our way to our current work through various stepping stones of service efforts—and the first stepping stone was a long way from where we are today.

GREATER AWARENESS OF SELF AND COMMUNITY

You'll also be surprised by how much you learn as you begin these small acts of service. First of all, you'll get a better understanding of what you uniquely have to offer. You might discover you have a knack for organizing the food pantry at the soup kitchen and seek out further opportunities where you can contribute your organizational talents. Or perhaps you're great at making kids laugh, something you don't have the opportunity to do at your nine-to-five job. You may also find out where you're not gifted—an equally important discovery as you determine next steps. Simply showing up and trying out a service opportunity helps develop greater understanding about where you'll be most effective, which in turn helps you make a greater impact.

Serving also helps you counter initial judgments you might feel about communities in need. Perhaps you've driven past lines of people waiting for food at a soup kitchen before, and have made assumptions about their lack of drive, or indulgence in addiction. However, if you start serving those people in the soup kitchen and ask to hear their stories, you'll likely realize that these people have much more in common with you than you expected. Putting names and stories to the faces on the street robs you of judgment, and gives you compassion instead. You begin connecting to communities of people previously outside your networks, and engage with them in meaningful ways.

Your eyes are also opened to the needs of your community and the complexity of its various issues, as Ken's anecdote can attest.

KEN'S STORY: THE BROWN SWEAT SUIT

As a young Sailor, I started my career in the Ceremonial Guard. When we performed a ceremony at the White House and Arlington Cemetery, we were given boxed lunches, each of which contained two cigarettes. At this time in the early 80s, just after the Vietnam War, there was a huge homeless population behind the White House, many of whom were veterans. We'd see them walking around on the streets picking up cigarette butts and smoking them. Most of us in the Ceremonial Guard didn't smoke, so I used to go around and collect everybody's cigarettes and leftover food, and then offer them to these homeless guys. Then I'd start talking to them.

I'll never forget one guy in particular named Charlie; he wore this brown sweat suit, day in and day out. It looked like it hadn't been washed in years—it was filthy. I was giving him food and cigarettes one day and said, "Hey, Charlie. That sweat suit's in bad shape, man. I've got a really nice blue one. Can I bring it to you on the next trip?"

He got very defensive and said, "Don't you take my sweat suit."

That moment made me realize that Charlie wasn't just a guy who didn't have a home—Charlie was mentally ill. I had a quick fix in mind, but that's not how service was going to work for him. When I asked that question, I realized that there was more to the story; he needed help beyond just getting a shower and a new sweat suit.

There's almost always more to the story than we see at first. There are areas of complexity that we can't see until we're right there, in it. Once we are "in it" though, we may start to understand the deeper needs of how best to help. Trying to serve without first understanding the full complexity of a situation is reckless, and recklessness occurs at all levels of our society.

BUILDING UP STAMINA

Simple engagement in small acts of service—regardless of your particular passion for what those might be—builds your spiritual wellness, just as weight-lifting in the gym builds your physical wellness. It's easy enough to see the benefits of habitually working out, and service likewise is worth making a habit; regular practice strengthens you.

Serving other people can be incredibly invigorating and can also be taxing. Take an experience like tutoring at-risk foster kids; each moment of headway is exciting and meaningful, but the kids may be challenging and act out. You might leave a session in this context feeling joyful about the laughs you shared, and simultaneously depressed about how many challenges these kids have ahead of them.

Wading into areas of need can be hard. Homeless people may depress you; physical labor may exhaust you; hospital visits may initially turn your stomach. However, there are also profound gifts to be found in each area of service, which make it worth enduring the challenges.

Recognize that you may not be able to change the world overnight. However, if you can impact somebody's life by contributing a few hours on a consistent basis, that's one of the greatest accomplishments you can ever achieve.

INPUT, NOT OUTCOME

We've talked about impact, accomplishments, and changing lives through serving. However, we believe it's important to focus more on what you put in, than on what you hope to get out.

Some of the world's most successful CEOs embody this principle. Steve Jobs started out simply wanting to make beautiful things; that initial input ended up leading to a company worth nearly a trillion dollars—but that's not where it began. Bill Gates originally started working with software because it was his passion. He wasn't focused on the outcome of becoming rich; he was led by what deeply mattered to him. Of course, he's become one of the world's richest men, but he continues to live life according to his principles, using his vast wealth to fund his far-reaching charitable organization.

Those who focus mainly on outcome often experience the reverse effect. They compromise their principles to accomplish an end. Even in cases where this method produces "success," there's typically dysfunction and dissatisfaction that goes along with it. "Success" worth achieving—whether through knowledge gained, or principled thriving—is an organic process that comes from good input.

"When I leave here on this earth, did I take more than I gave? Did I look after other people or did I do it all for fame?"[41]

—MACKLEMORE, "GLORIOUS"

Viktor Frankl, author of *Man's Search for Meaning*, addresses this concept as well. He makes the point that happiness and success ensue as the result of you following your conscience—and that simply pursuing happiness and success as the end goal doesn't work.[42] We believe you must find the problem you have to solve and solve it: *that's* the start of a meaningful life.

Don't take on the world yet, but take on a small corner. At some stage in the game, we hope that you can give back on a much larger level, something we'll address in our final chapter.

JOSH'S STORY: PASSION FOUND IN AN UNEXPECTED PLACE

After leaving my corporate executive job, I went to work for Mort for about a year; I ran a technology start-up for him, and a lot of my work focused on studying the science of happiness. It was an ironic place for me to be at the time. I was dealing with anxiety, depression, and feeling suicidal, while reading books and research about how to be happy in Mort's family office.

One day, Mort took us to a food bank to spend some time serving. I remember being in line with him, putting boxes together—and for a few hours, I forgot about myself. The experience gave me a bounce. I was able to make a contribution that was in support of somebody else, not just me. I had tried finding this bounce in various unhealthy ways, but nowhere else was it as pure as what I experienced helping somebody else in a meaningful, respectful way.

After I got back from my trip around the world, I started seeking out other ways to serve—though admittedly, I hadn't yet realized the importance of getting healthy myself. I'd been told by a friend of mine that there was a suicidal veteran struggling at a VA hospital in Texas who could use support. At this point, I didn't know any veterans, but I agreed to reach out to him. I sent him a couple books, and then we talked over email. Eventually, I decided to go see him. We ended up spending the day together, playing Frisbee-golf and going bowling. The experience made us both feel more human—it enabled us to put aside some of the labels we'd been dragging around: "suicidal," "depressed," and so on. We were just two ordinary people.

For me, that's where the discovery of my passion started. It felt profoundly meaningful to do something that offered someone a sense of dignity, a sense of pride, a sense of care. As I sought to recreate my life, I tried out various new wellness practices as I've mentioned, but I also explored different areas to serve. Essentially, I was "dating myself," exposing myself to new ideas and pursuits, trying to discover what resonated with me.

I would have never believed you if you'd told me I would end up working with combat veterans who were struggling with PTSD. But somehow, by following the breadcrumb trail of the work that intrigued me and satisfied me, I was led to where I am now. I remained open to new possibilities and ideas, and I knew I wanted to be engaged in service. That approach ended up leading to a huge departure from the path that I was on—and now, I can confidently say that I intend to dedicate the remainder of my life to training people to achieve Posttraumatic Growth and teaching them how to *struggle well*. Somehow, I found the right path.

Humility is a crucial component to getting there. I needed

the willingness to ask for help, and I had to recognize that my current approach wasn't working. I also had to be humble enough to listen to the various teachers I encountered along the way—guys like Mort, Ken, and Dusty. They showed me how to help myself in critical ways before headlong pursuing a life of service.

Recently, Ken and I sat with a guy who was going to kill himself only three weeks prior. To see him laughing, joyous, curious, and excited, was amazing. By sharing our own strengths and experiences, we had the privilege of helping awaken another human being who was on the precipice of death.

A friend of mine says that the two greatest human needs are the need to grow and the need to contribute. I've found my way into a life that enables me to do both—and it's incredible.

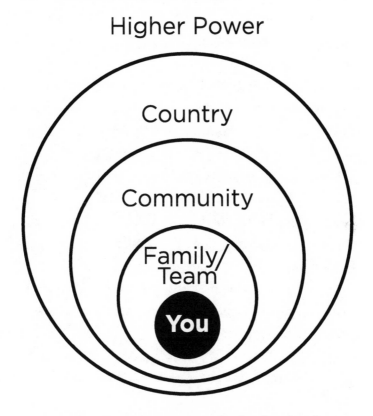

In our work with veterans, we emphasize that there's a correct order in who you should focus on helping first, which we represent using concentric circles. At the core of the four circles is you: you must first help yourself, before you can help others. The next circle represents your family and "team," i.e., your three-to-five support network. After you've achieved health in your closest community, you're able to move to the next circle, your wider community. Beyond that lies the much larger service opportunities to your nation.

As you walk this road of Posttraumatic Growth, you want to engage in service at a level proportionate to where you're at. If you overdo the service before you're in a healthy place, you'll experience diminishing returns. Your self-care will be neglected, and you'll end up back where you started—a place that won't allow you to effectively care for anyone, not even yourself. Do serve—but do it in a way that's smart, healthy for all, and sustainable.

There are no shortcuts in life. When you try to go from Point A to D, instead of A, B, C, and D, something will surely go wrong. Struggling well is about sustained transformation. The only way you do that is by doing it right: with diligence, deliberateness, and discipline, moving slowly to enhance your health in one area of life, before moving to the next.

BEGIN WITH YOU

Many want to plunge into service as an escape from struggle—it feels like a quick fix out of inner turmoil. You might see this in someone who tries to escape his problems by becoming a monk, or someone who throws off every aspect of her life by moving to India and working at Save the Children—or even someone who dives into pursuing a counseling degree because of their own internal chaos. Attempts like these would all fall into that category of spiritual bypass. The phrase describes the attempt to shortcut a necessary process: the deep, introspective journey of self-healing.

We've encountered countless veterans who struggle after getting out of the military, and invest all their time and energy into serving other people. They end up a wreck; they've built up no capacity to regulate themselves so they end up being ineffective in their service to other people and of no service to themselves.

One veteran we knew was seriously struggling, yet he was going to college during the day and to the YMCA every night. He was mentoring kids on the weekends as well. He so struggled being on his own that he poured all his anxiety into trying to help other people. Those other people became his drug, which was dangerous both for him and the people he was trying to help. If you don't take care of yourself first, it's nearly impossible to take care of others well.

The pendulum can swing from being totally self-focused, to being totally others-focused. Seek balance and the self-awareness to recognize what you need. When you're struggling, you want to be more on the self-focused side; eventually, you'll want to build a balanced life where the pendulum rests in the middle. Moving slowly through these concentric circles ensures you get into the practice of taking care of yourself so you can take care of others.

As you do so, keep an eye on your Wellness Triangle. How are you doing in your different categories of wellness? Are your acts of service helping to inflate the ball in the center of your triangle while you make progress in the other areas, or are other areas suffering as a result?

"Progress" is the key word here. You'll likely need to start investing in the next concentric circle even before all of your Wellness Triangle scores are at a "five," simply because life moves on. You can't turn the clocks off for the next several weeks while you pull your life together. However, if you see steady progress in your Wellness Triangle categories, you've started serving in small ways, and you see an increased ability to self-regulate—then, you're likely ready to move out into the next ring of serving your family and friends.

FAMILY AND TEAM

When we talk about investment in your family and team, we're once again referring to the three-to-five people with whom you spend the most time. For most of the book, we've discussed ways for you to lean on this community for support. However, the best relationships are mutually beneficial. For this reason, it's important for you to be offering support to this community, not just taking it. For a community to thrive, everybody needs to put in their hard work and contribution—including you.

True, you might be struggling; true, your progress in the Wellness Triangle categories may be slow. But that doesn't mean you have nothing to offer.

If you've been isolating yourself from the people who most love you during this struggle, your honest communication may be a profound gift. Honesty builds trust, and trust is what builds strong, mutually beneficial relationships. Therefore, the first, best thing you may have to offer your family and friends might simply be transparency. It's likely that your story may even liberate somebody else in your three-to-five to acknowledge their own challenges.

Ideally, your three-to-five network will give you opportunities to be both student and teacher; you'll eventually have an influence on the people that most influence you. If your closest community ultimately arrives on a similar path as you, you're in a group of people who are all primed and equipped to help each other through life.

We have a friend who has struggled in his relationship with his son for some time. The son would likely benefit from some nurturing investment from his dad, but our friend has started investing in another kid entirely. He's taken on a Big Brother role and is now putting his time toward that relationship, trying to fix what he feels like he's ruined with his son. His motivations may be understandable, but he's putting his own family and the life of the kid he's mentoring at risk. Clearly, there are some problems within himself and his own family that need healing before he tries to serve other people.

It's examples like this that make us believe so strongly in the right order of service laid out in the concentric circles. Rather than trying to make yourself feel better by diving into community service *away* from your family, take your family with you to the "small stuff" service projects we laid out in the previous section. Bring your kids along to the soup kitchen and let them see you serving others. Have a good conversation with them afterwards about the importance of what you did together.

Service starts at home. Perhaps you push growth in this area by making time to play with your kids every Saturday for two hours, or calling your grandmother. Plan date nights with your spouse or outings with your best friend. Put in your contribution to build up the network that you value most.

COMMUNITY

Three important developments start to occur as you move through the first two concentric circles. First, you'll see increased health and strength in your own life. As your Wellness Triangle sharpens, and the "spiritual wellness" ball within it inflates, you'll experience more space for self-regulation and balance. Secondly, you'll experience greater joy within your three-to-five network as you begin prioritizing investment in the people you most care about. That, too, leads to greater balance and fulfillment in your life.

The third development ideally leads you into the third concentric circle, that of your community. As you sense that you've got more to give, you should put that new energy into action. Participating in "small stuff" service will likely open your eyes to areas where you feel passionate about serving. You'll start to see ways your service, or that of an organization, could expand—and you may feel inspired to lead that expansion.

We know of a young man in Portland, Oregon who was moved to start serving the large homeless population in the city. He started off by doing small acts of kindness with the homeless, providing them food. Then he began thinking, "How do we sustain this? Who's going to give us money to continue to provide food for these people?" He went on to create a business that made meals you didn't have to heat up. For every meal they sold, they were able to give one away, similar to the model of Tom's Shoes. Like anyone, this young man probably had some personal struggles and wisely elected to start small. However, as he got to better understand the issue, he was able to apply his brainpower to help problem-solve, expand his level of service, and create sustainability.

Service starts with time and muscle power. You show up, and you help a hurricane victim clean out her kitchen. You show up, and you fill up boxes at a food bank. You show up, and you help bathe animals at the humane society. Sometimes, that's as far as it goes. Other times, you discover an area of service that draws you in and inspires you to do more.

Service *continues*, therefore, with deeper investment, where we begin to embody the belief that we are one another's keepers. We step aside from a lifestyle of self-centeredness, and start experiencing the deep fulfillment that comes from helping our fellow human beings. This attitude and approach represents what makes our nation different, and reminds us all that the true strength of our nation comes from strong, healthy communities.

Every Community Has Needs

Ken lives in the richest county in the United States: Loudoun County, Virginia. When cost of living is factored in, per household, Loudoun County has the highest median take-home income in the nation. And yet, the county still has massive needs.

Loudoun has a massive food bank issue. It has a heroin problem. There are MS-13 gangs in the county. There's an abused women's shelter in need of beds, along with abused children's shelters; there's a boys' home that can't raise enough money to keep the lights on—and this is in the wealthiest county in the United States. What does this tell us? There is literally nowhere in the country where communities don't need help.

One man within our community, Rick, experienced the deep personal tragedy of losing his wife to cancer.[43] His wife had been prescribed numerous opioids to help her manage her pain, and not all of those prescriptions were cleaned out when she passed away. The man's nineteen-year-old daughter began taking some of her mother's medication to cope with her own grief, ultimately becoming addicted. Although she sought treatment from a psychiatrist, she couldn't break free from her addiction. Her life spiraled downward. Just before her twenty-sixth birthday, she overdosed and died.

Rick's grief is enormous—and yet, he showed tremendous strength in his response to the deaths of his wife and daughter. On a Loudon County website, he writes, "Six days after my daughter died, I saw an article in the paper about a program out of the local sheriff's office. He is trying to raise awareness about the local opioid crisis. He wants people to know that heroin is easy to find in our region and inexpensive to boot...But, too often the response [in our community] is, 'There isn't a problem here.' As a society, we are in complete denial."

Rick started volunteering with the Sheriff's office and ultimately expanded his role to serve as one of their speakers, sharing his story. He writes, "I just hope that before I die, one person approaches me to say, 'I heard you speak, and you helped me. That would help me make sense of a senseless tragedy and to do my part to End the Need in Loudoun."

This man faced huge adversity and ultimately determined his response needed to be one of action. He decided to do something about the problem that plagued him, and is now sharing his story to help others within his local community.

Ronald Reagan's philanthropic initiative in the 80s aimed to bring philanthropy from a federal level to the community level. He believed the people "on the ground" within local areas were best equipped to address their community's unique struggles. We agree with that assessment. Large-scale disasters often attract our attention and sympathy; examples like the 2017 hurricane in Houston inspired people from around the country to hop in their cars and drive to Texas to help. Their efforts are laudable, but you don't have to drive across the country to serve. Your local community needs you just as much as the people of Houston.

"Clicktivism" has become popular in recent years—we are happy to loudly vocalize our support or disapproval of various efforts online, but far less likely to take action in those areas with our time, muscles, or brainpower. Rather than watching the news at home and throwing your slippers at the TV out of anger, or writing nasty posts on Facebook, consider how you can take action on that issue at the community level.

Just as we've recommended practices to help you prepare yourself for struggle, communities need similar investment. If a community is able to proactively build up its infrastructure, food banks, blood banks, and so on, then when a natural disaster hits—it's prepared.

Particularly in the nonprofit world, problems need real brainpower. Service efforts need the sustainability mindset of the business world or the logistical savvy of engineers. Chances are, you have an area of expertise that a nonprofit could benefit from; you have resources—whether through volunteerism, donating money, building partnerships, or lending expertise—which are needed. As you start to find your passion through small acts of service, ask yourself, "How can I apply my brainpower from everything I've learned and try to solve this problem?"

"Serve and solve."[44]

—BRIDGESPAN, A NONPROFIT CONSULTING COMPANY

When confronted with a problem in your own community,

it's common sense that the problem, ideally, would be eradicated—not perpetuated. Some nonprofits put out the worst fires, but don't develop models that will lead to long-term, permanent solutions. Yet with understanding and intelligent problem-solving, it is possible to solve these issues through smart service. There's a tremendous opportunity to harness the remarkable collection of skills that exist in every community to make a meaningful impact on its struggles.

An individual who is struggling is not so different from a community that struggles. They both need the same thing: hope and opportunities to grow. We're not necessarily recommending you quit your job and go work at a nonprofit. However, if you can be efficient and effective with the time you spend, you can make a real impact on healing a community's issues, just as you work on healing yourself. Start small and build.

And then keep building.

NATION

Some people experience a great deal of success with their service efforts. Their passion and expertise collide beautifully, leading them not only into personal fulfillment, but also into an enormously productive model. People in this position may be ready to make a nationwide impact.

What does that look like? Maybe you scale your service model up so that it addresses a problem on a wider scale—for instance, moving from a community program that involves safe disposal of hypodermic needles, to a larger program that combats drug addiction in a number of ways. Maybe you go from serving politically at a community level, to pursuing politics in the US House of Representatives or the Senate. If people have arrived here after first moving through the other concentric circles, they will be making these large-scale decisions with an understanding of themselves, their close network, and their "main street" community.

Unfortunately, not everyone serving our country on a national level has achieved this depth of understanding. A common, but destructive path leads people to drive themselves to the outer ring as a result of their egos, without first developing a healthy understanding of the inner concentric circles. Real damage starts to occur when people make national level policies and programs without understanding the critical elements of local community issues. These people are not congruent; they have no genuine individual health, and yet they believe they can help others.

George H.W. Bush is a great example of a leader who took on the mantle of power for the right reasons, after first moving through the smaller stages of service. He ultimately pursued the presidency because he felt he had a responsibility to give back, after experiencing privilege in his own life. His inaugural address reflects the humility and integrity he practiced while in office, especially as it relates to his beliefs about the importance of serving others:

"America is never wholly herself unless she is engaged in high moral principle. We as a people have such a purpose today. It is to make kinder the face of the Nation and gentler the face of the world. My friends, we have work to do. There are the homeless, lost and roaming. There are the children who have nothing, no love and no normalcy. There are those who cannot free themselves of enslavement to whatever addiction—drugs, welfare, the demoralization that rules the slums. There is crime to be conquered, the rough crime of the streets. There are young women to be helped who are about to become mothers of children they can't care for and might not love...The old ideas are new again because they're not old, they are timeless: duty, sacrifice, commitment, and a patriotism that finds its expression in taking part and pitching in."[45]

—GEORGE H.W. BUSH

George H.W. Bush's words emphasize the importance of servant-leadership. Imagine the effectiveness and sustainable progress that might be accomplished in our nation if our leaders were all driven by integrity, humility, and compassion—not ego.

We believe you're ready to serve nationally when you know you have value to add, and you don't need credit for what you accomplish. If you seek to serve on a national level, you've got to have the willpower, the staying power, and the sustainability to support your position, otherwise you won't be successful.

PATIENT, SLOW PROGRESS

Healthy service starts by helping the person in front of you—and when you're standing in front of the mirror, that first person is yourself. Then, you help the people right beside you. Eventually, your scope broadens, but it starts by simply asking, "What's the need?" When you identify a need, and start to seek out ways to help, meaningful service becomes natural.

"Fill yourselves first and then only will you be able to give to others."

—ATTRIBUTED TO SAINT AUGUSTINE

The drowning can't save the drowning. In our own work, we've learned that we'll be at our maximum capacity to serve others well if we're taking care of ourselves—it's the reason Josh journals, meditates, and works out every morning before coming to work. We endorse these ideas because we've lived them, and have seen the effectiveness of these principles in others. When your own foundation is strong, you have a strong basis to engage and support other people.

In walking this road from struggle to strength—especially when it comes to service—patience is crucial. We often see people complete the first seven-day stretch of our eighteen-month program, and they experience hope they haven't felt in a long time. Often, they feel ready to put that new energy toward giving back, but we urge them to put it first toward their own healing. We're constantly coaching our participants to be respectful, patient, and kind to themselves, while also being kind to others. This journey takes time.

Imagine getting your first paycheck after a long stretch of unemployment. You might feel great getting that cash in your wallet, but you'll put yourself right back in the hole if you go out and spend it. Instead, the smart thing to do is invest the money in your own savings account and get yourself on firmer financial ground. Once you've built up a financial cushion, you'll be in a place to give to others. The same concept is true in this area of service.

Once again, we return to the concept of balance. Just as you want to live within the boundaries of the sine wave, you want to maintain a balance of self-care and service to others. This balance helps you respond to stressful moments that may come up during service, rather than reacting.

Remember the barometer you have in your Wellness Triangle. If you're honest with yourself as you regularly evaluate your progress in Wellness Triangle categories, you'll have a clear picture of your growth and stability. Are you moving closer toward your goals each day, each week, each month? If so, then you're building a sense of momentum that's great to share with other people; you can bring people with you on that journey. Use the wellness practices in this book as your mirror to determine whether or not you're getting to a healthier place.

Consider also your motivation for service. Are you doing this for you, or for the people you want to help? If you seek out service because you want to be of use to other people—that's a sign of healthy motivation. However, if you're serving mainly as an effort to refill your own tank, you're likely attempting spiritual bypass. Stop, and do some intentional personal work before trying to go any further. Trust us, service done right makes you feel great.

In the context of service, the opposite of balance can make you a martyr: you become somebody who gives everything you have to serve everyone else. And then, you have nothing left—except probably a healthy dose of resentment.

Mother Teresa is a legendary woman of service who devoted her life to helping the poor in Calcutta; there's no argument that her efforts accomplished enormous good. However, letters discovered after her death revealed that she struggled with profound inner turmoil. In one letter, she wrote, "Darkness surrounds me on all sides. I can't lift my soul to God. No light or inspiration enters my soul. Heaven? What emptiness, not a single thought of Heaven enters my mind, for there is no hope. The place of God in my soul is blank."[46] Although we can't know the complexities of Mother's Teresa's psyche, we can see that her life prioritized others, always. It seems obvious that she put her physical self at risk during her years of service—and perhaps her efforts took their toll emotionally and spiritually as well.

Very few of us have the strength of Mother Teresa to endure years of service while carrying such profound personal darkness. We believe the most sustainable efforts start with taking care of yourself, and then other people. Struggling well and living well require sustained transformation, not spurts of energy that quickly die out.

Remember the minefield. Dig down deep, and identify the dangers you're dealing with. Take time to clear each mine, tracking your steady progress forward. Once that field is clear, go back and lead others through it. You're now equipped to show them the way.

CHAPTER SEVEN

GUIDING OTHERS

———

"For, while the tale of how we suffer, and how we are delighted, and how we may triumph is never new, it always must be heard. There isn't any other tale to tell, it's the only light we've got in all this darkness."[47]

—JAMES BALDWIN

When you started reading this book, maybe you didn't even know your darkness was there. But then you spotted it: the cave. Its mouth yawned open, dark, and foreboding. There was a promise of treasure inside, but guaranteed risk as well. What would you find in there?

It's likely the struggles you're currently enduring have not yet ended. As we've written, the journey from struggle to strength is a long one. If there's one hope we have for you in reading this final chapter though, it's that you've made the decision to venture into your cave of treasures. One step in: gathering your companions for support and developing wellness practices for protection and guidance. Another step in: confronting your past and shining a light deep into the dark. A third step in: you've made a plan and a route—goals to guide your steps and progress. A fourth: you gain the firm footing you need to help the people behind you. So your journey through Posttraumatic Growth continues.

Maybe you haven't collected all the treasures to be found in your cave yet, but you can see them glimmering within your reach. Those treasures appear in five different areas. The one closest to you appears in the form of deeper relationships with other people. As you develop the willingness to be open about your experiences and your struggles, you experience greater authenticity and depth in your relationships. You also carry with you the mark of the struggler; people see in you a common sense of empathy that comes from having been there and done it—and they're more willing to share their stories with you as a result. As you travel further into the cave, you gain a greater sense of your personal strength, a treasure all its own. You know that no matter what you encounter in your life, you'll have the strength not simply to endure it, but to thrive because of it.

Deeper within the cave, another treasure awaits you—small, but indescribably beautiful. This one takes the form of gratitude. You have an appreciation for life that delights in the smallest things, from the capacity to wake up each day and breathe, to the smaller joys of flowers and nature. Near this treasure lies another one: a zest for new possibilities, a desire to find out more about yourself and the world, and a constant sense of curiosity about life.

Above you, dusting the cave ceiling in glittering folds, is another gift. In terms of spiritual and existential change, you begin to reflect on the deeper meaning of life and its purpose. Certainly we've shared a number of different ideas about why we're all here. We believe one of our main purposes in life is to leave a reason for why we lived. We're here to struggle well and to figure out who we are. We do that with people, using practices and principles.

Often, it's struggle that pushes us into the cave we fear to enter. With no other options, that becomes the only way forward—and what an opportunity that is. We're forced to live life at a deeper and more profound level than ever before. We carry a sense of authenticity that we never could have accessed previously. And although the treasures found on the journey are not gems that can be touched, they're the most valuable gifts we could ever possess. Perhaps best of all, we have the opportunity to help other people travel the road from struggle to strength, the ultimate form of service in allowing other people to achieve Posttraumatic Growth.

It's this last gift we want to focus on in this final chapter:

guiding others along this journey. The science of PTG shows that people who have experienced struggle and their own Posttraumatic Growth are the best people to help others—in that way, PTG is inherently democratic. This means anybody can do it; the only prerequisite is that you've made your own journey.

SUCCESS IN TERMS OF POSTTRAUMATIC GROWTH

So how do you know if you've "made it," on this journey from struggle to strength? You can't look for the end of struggle as confirmation of your success on this journey; as we've repeated, struggle is guaranteed to continue for the rest of your life. Then how do you measure success in terms of Posttraumatic Growth?

Given that struggle occurs throughout life, PTG is essentially a lifelong journey. However, there are some "successful" travelers who are ready to be Expert Guides to help others begin the journey. These people have mastered the understanding of the Posttraumatic Growth framework and the outcomes associated with that framework. A person gets there through the five phases of education, regulation, disclosure, creating a positive story, and serving others. In this book, we've done our best to walk you through each phase.

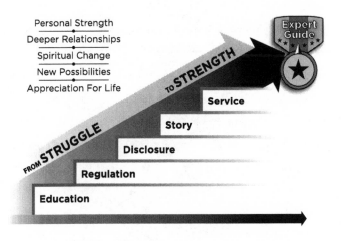

We hope we've educated you on the opportunities that can be found within struggle, and reinforced the fact that struggle is with you all through life. We've talked about self-regulation practices that help you respond, rather than react to new challenges in life. We discussed disclosure in Chapters Three and Four, and ways to create your positive new story in Chapter Five. And throughout this process, we've recommended the value of carrying out small acts of service to others.

Another way to envision someone who's achieved success in terms of PTG is to think of a mountain climber. When engulfed in struggle, you start deep in a valley, looking up at what feels like an impossibly high summit. But going through these phases enables you—slowly, steadily—to climb higher and higher. Eventually, you find yourself standing on the summit of Mount Struggle. The fact that struggle exists in your life now is no longer particularly relevant. You've accepted its presence, you understand how to deal with it, and you've learned how to build a reservoir of capacity and strength.

From the summit, it's easy to see the rest of the mountain range that lies ahead of you; there will be plenty more challenges to face in the future. But you have new confidence that you can take them on; you've learned how to climb a mountain.

An "Expert Guide" is someone who is equipped to lead another person through the process of struggle to strength. These people have "summited" Mount Struggle, and are ready to do one of the next, hardest steps: coming back down the mountain and leading others back up. Expert Guides enable other people to travel that hard journey, supporting them and guiding them in a way that honors each person's dignity and unique story. Expert Guides step away from a self-centered existence and serve others.

CHARACTERISTICS OF AN EXPERT GUIDE

An Expert Guide is congruent. It is only when the head and heart are connected, and thoughts, feelings, and actions are positively aligned, that one can respond to life, rather than react to it. This state called "congruence" is cultivated by regular wellness practices, a strong support network (your three-to-five) that provides accountability, and living a service-oriented life. Expert Guides lead from the front, through their experience, actions, and way of being, not just their words.

An Expert Guide is honest in a world that can often be indirect and passive-aggressive. Being direct is rare and valuable. This honesty—"saying what you mean, meaning what you say, and never saying it mean"—is characteristic of what it means to be an Expert Guide.

An Expert Guide listens and rarely misses the opportunity to remain silent. A willingness to listen without forming a response, seeking to judge, or problem-solve, is seen as the main distinction between Expert Guides and other people in life. In a world of talkers, listening deeply to another human being and bearing witness to his or her struggles and concerns is one of the highest forms of service. Listening is one of the keys to connecting with others and it's a skill that must be practiced and cultivated.

An Expert Guide is open. The capacity and willingness to share lessons, experiences, and struggles honestly is what makes Guides successful and allows them to lead from the front. Guides who share openly and effectively have made peace with their past experiences so they can share in a healthy and effective manner. Guides also recognize the importance of serving as both teacher and student, always remaining open to learning from the experiences of others.

An Expert Guide is patient. Every human being is on a journey at their own pace and in their own way. Guides must meet people where they are at, and trust in the journey that they're on. In the words of Congressman John Lewis, "Firecrackers go off in a flash, then leave nothing but ashes. I prefer a pilot light—the flame is nothing flashy, but once it is lit, it doesn't go out. It burns steadily, and it burns forever."[48] Be the slow, steady, patient pilot light in the lives of the people you're guiding.

An Expert Guide shows positive regard. At times, people can be challenging and frustrating. No matter what, maintaining positive regard is paramount, recognizing that people are struggling human beings seeking a better path and a better life.

An Expert Guide is prepared. Years of exploration and development created the model we've laid out in this book, and an Expert Guide takes the time to learn, practice, and deeply understand it. This preparation enhances a Guide's ability to deliver that content to the people who need it.

An Expert Guide is fully present. No one is immune from the ups and downs of life, including Expert Guides. Events and challenges arise in life that are distracting and force deeper dives into the guide's well-being. Guides must devote all of their time, attention, and effort to the people they're working with. That means your cell phone is put away, your mind is focused, and you're fully engaged in every moment.

An Expert Guide is curious. Every human being has a story to tell and deserves the opportunity to share it. Guides should ask thought-provoking questions and minimize talking. It's far more powerful when people being guided can recognize their *own* capacity to help themselves and others.

Life is not hard; it is hard work. Living well and struggling well requires humility, regular and intentional Wellness Practices, a strong support network, and the setting and accomplishing of goals. We encourage Expert Guides to be honorable, gracious, supportive, authentic, and to never miss a golden opportunity to be quiet and listen.

GUIDES ARE NEEDED

You may have read the list of Expert Guide characteristics and are ready to close the book on this chapter: "Too much work; not for me. I'd rather enjoy my own summit experience, and let others figure it out on their own."

If you're anywhere near this thought though—consider

this. Did *you* do it on your own? Were you entirely alone in your journey, or were there others who made sacrifices to help you along? Even if you received no help other than this book, you did indeed receive help from others. And if you've applied any of our recommendations in this book, it's likely you sought out the help of others as well.

Or perhaps you read those characteristics and thought, "I'm definitely not there yet." Fair enough; becoming an Expert Guide is the pinnacle of the PTG journey, and it takes much more time to live out that journey than it typically does to read a book.

Let us encourage all our readers to shoot for this pinnacle though. Our world badly needs people who are willing and equipped to lead others from struggle to strength. In 2016, over 64,000 people died from drug overdoses, and we're on track to beat that record moving forward.[49] We live in a world where far too many people believe that their tomorrows will be worse than their yesterdays, where they experience a lack of meaning and purpose. Far too many people don't have any sense of hope that they can change their own fate; they believe they are merely a victim of their circumstances.

Everywhere we look, the numbers seem to be getting worse. The US reports a thirty-year high in the civilian suicide rate, and a forty-year high in the suicide rate for young girls.[50] The US also has an opioid epidemic that's ravaging the country. Clearly, there are countless people suffering from wounds that cannot be seen but can certainly be felt.

If you have experienced any struggle in your own story, you might be able to understand the importance of treating others with kindness. We can't know the invisible wounds people carry. Some of the worst perpetrators of road rage are veterans who are haunted by memories of feeling trapped in enemy territory, and they remember losing friends in battle. It's easy to write someone off as an asshole, but you don't know why a person might act out the way they do. Normally, it's because they have a story.

People often make assumptions about other people's relative states of well-being based on the outside of their Wellness Triangles—on what we can see. However, as Josh's story reveals, this exterior view rarely provides the whole picture; in fact, in Josh's case, the flashy exterior of his life masked the misery he carried on the inside. If that's true for someone who looks like they have it all together, how much more must a person be struggling who reveals a crumbling outer Wellness Triangle? We are all in need of patience and compassion.

The world isn't about you as an individual; it's about all of us getting along and doing our best to live well, and struggle well. Our belief in growth depends on the idea that you are not wedded to the way you are. You're simply how you have been trained to be. When you experience the new possibilities offered by this knowledge in your own personal life, it's a reminder of what's possible when you apply that same point of view to the world. You can achieve tremendous growth out of great suffering and struggle—provided that you're shown the way.

When you've endured a grueling pathway to strength, you want to keep other people from having to experience struggle in the destructive way you may have experienced. The idea that we suffer so others don't is as old as humankind. It's the basis of Christianity, which believes that Jesus suffered so those who have faith in him don't have to. Judaism takes up this belief as well. The Jews were slaves in Egypt and made their way to the Holy Land, suffering so that future generations didn't have to. They were freed from slavery, and we can free ourselves, likewise, from the slavery of our minds. If you've experienced that liberation, then you may be uniquely qualified to help others find freedom as well.

SHARING YOUR STORY AS AN EXPERT GUIDE

Imagine a whole world of people struggling under the burdens of enormous, heavy rucksacks. What if you could see the weights people carry? You'd understand why so many walk hunched over and struggle to make progress. Essentially, that *is* our world—but no one acknowledges the rucksacks. People collectively pretend they're not there, and no one asks questions about why everyone walks so slowly and painfully.

As an Expert Guide, you can offer someone profound freedom when you call out the weight in your own rucksack. By willingly telling your story, people are freed to acknowledge the weights they carry too. When there is a burden on your back, be honest with others about the fact that it's there. Tell them what it is. Do it nicely. Do it kindly. Do it earnestly and authentically.

There's a right way and a wrong way to share your story. Told correctly, your story can inspire others to share their own stories, and they can begin to heal. Told badly, it will draw people into your past trauma and cause you to relive it. We'll explain the difference in methods of sharing.

EXPOSURE

Exposure describes a method of sharing your story unwillingly. You're put on the spot and called upon to expose your hardest stories before you feel safe. You share because you feel like you must, not because you're ready or willing to do so.

This method of sharing is unhealthy. It's one of the reasons we suggest sharing your story with a trusted friend even before a counselor, because some mental health therapists ask for this kind of painful information before establishing a relationship of trust with their clients.

When you share unwillingly, you feel exposed. You may end up reliving painful experiences. Furthermore, there's no control or self-mastery over telling your story. It's not your choice, and you're unable to regulate the emotions that may emerge.

Although it's sometimes important to do things that scare you, in general, we strongly believe sharing your story should happen when *you* choose to share it—in other words, not through "exposure."

DISCLOSURE

We've discussed disclosure extensively in this book. However, for the sake of distinguishing this method of sharing, we'll make some clear distinctions.

As opposed to exposure, disclosure is a choice. Sharing your story may still bring up strong emotions and look or feel messy—that's okay. You need to start somewhere. But whereas "exposure" feels like something you're forced into, disclosure describes your own willingness to share, knowing that doing so leads you to greater understanding.

Disclosure is also different from the final category of sharing we'll describe as self-mastery. Self-mastery in sharing your story implies that you can treat it with total objectivity and a degree of emotional removal. People in the disclosure phase are not there yet, simply because it takes time before your hardest experiences have lost their emotional power over you. The first several times you share your story may still produce an emotionally charged experience; the first time anyone takes a close look at the hard experiences in their past, it's bound to stir that up. If you face suffering and tears, it's because you're doing the hard act of working through it and facing it.

Disclosure is an unloading experience; it's getting the weight off your back. As we described earlier in the book, disclosure often ushers in a profound change in people when they choose to do it. Disclosure also describes a more comprehensive sharing. Rather than offering up snippets of your life here and there, disclosure describes a fuller, longer telling of your story that helps both you and your listeners connect the dots between your past experiences and present state. In this way, the process helps build self-awareness and understanding. As discussed in Chapter Four, it's something that's done in an intentional setting, with an intentional audience.

SELF-MASTERY

Expert Guides are those who can share their stories with self-mastery. When you've achieved self-mastery in telling your story, you possess several key characteristics.

Objectivity

The first few times you share your story, it may be hard, emotional, and leave you feeling drained. Eventually however, sharing your story will start to feel like second nature. Some people are able to share about traumatic events from their childhood as though they're talking about their favorite sports team. Somehow, they've been able to separate out the emotion and reach a place of calm objectivity. They don't relive their story while telling it; there's no body language that indicates tension, stress, or sadness. Instead, their telling seems characterized by curiosity and acceptance, rather than emotion.

This curiosity stems from the fact that their story has been explored and mined for meaning. Expert Guides can begin to express an understanding for why their trauma happened. They can talk about those experiences with peace; the experiences may not have been healthy, but the perspective of the person sharing is healthy. There's an understanding that these experiences were harmful in some ways, and in other ways, positive. They've moved forward and are no longer defined by their past.

Viktor Frankl embodies this perspective when he spoke about his experience in Nazi concentration camps:

"Once the meaning of suffering had been revealed to us, we refused to minimize or alleviate the camp's tortures by ignoring them or harboring false illusions and entertaining artificial optimism. Suffering had become a task on which we did not want to turn our backs. We had realized its hidden opportunities for achievement, the opportunities, which caused the poet Rilke to write, 'How much suffering there is to get through.' Rilke spoke of 'getting through suffering' as others would talk of 'getting through work.' There was plenty of suffering for us to get through. Therefore, it was necessary to face up to the full amount of suffering, trying to keep moments of weakness and furtive tears to a minimum. There was no need to be ashamed of tears, for tears bore witness that man had the greatest courage, the courage to suffer."[51]

—VIKTOR FRANKL, *MAN'S SEARCH FOR MEANING*

The Expert Guide mentality illustrates Frankl's point: struggle is useful, and life is life's best teacher. Recognizing this enables you to get to the point where you can look back on your story as a series of tests, lessons, and experiences that you were meant to understand, so that you can productively share your experiences as you move forward.

One of the Expert Guides at our retreat, Paul, willingly talks about his childhood even though his story contains shocking and horrible experiences. But Paul can share his story peacefully and objectively. He doesn't shut down emotionally, and he's able to talk about his experiences in a way that's compassionate to himself and the people in his story. He understands.

You'll know you've achieved objectivity in sharing your story if you can talk about it almost as though it happened to a different person—a previous version of yourself. You are able to discuss the other people in your story with objectivity, not with blame or judgment; you can genuinely express compassion for yourself and others. You don't judge your past or what you used to do; you're just explaining your journey.

Go First

Expert guides can help people shift from an exposure mentality to a disclosure mentality, simply by sharing their own stories first. Within our program, the two of us always share our own stories first to create an environment of safety and trust. As we do, we see people relax and ease into a posture of openness.

It's the same reason we've made a point to share our own stories with you throughout the book. We want *you*, also, to know you're not alone in your struggle. Mutual disclosure is powerful in stark contrast to the one-sided method of exposure. We've tried to help you create a clear picture, to inspire you, and to encourage you to be willing to follow these hard recommendations by sharing how those steps looked in our own lives.

When someone is willing to go first in sharing hard content—when someone goes out there and goes big—that person creates space for others to conclude, "This is a place of honesty. I get to leave stuff here because this person already did."

The same thing happens when a trail guide leads people up a mountain; the guide goes first. If you're acting as a guide during a group disclosure session, before you ask anyone else to do the "My Old Story" exercise, you'll do your own. You'll explain your M.O.S. to others first, with the purpose of giving them confidence, strength, and the courage to be open and honest.

Your willingness to talk about hard experiences liberates other people from the prison that they live in—you show them they don't have to pretend they don't have their own heavy rucksacks on their backs. You can give people permission to struggle and permission to get unstuck from where they might be.

Share with the Intention to Help

When you have self-mastery over your story, you can use it as a practical tool for helping others. You're able to use it to maximum effect by emphasizing or de-emphasizing parts as needed. In other words, you don't go into a room full of young kids and talk about feeling suicidal. You know your audience and understand where they're at. You're able to use your experiences to help move your listeners where they want to go or need to go next.

You also have to put your ego aside. Share when appropriate and hold back when needed. You're not trying to get somebody else to live your life; you're trying to share your experience, strength, and hope, to ensure that another person is better equipped to achieve Posttraumatic Growth.

There's a necessary humility that needs to be in place in order to utilize your story to its maximum effect—you need to get over what *you* might want to say. Instead, consider: what do the people in the room need to hear? What are they concerned about? After considering the answers to those questions, you're able to determine the best way to proceed. Your story can affect others in profound ways, and you own that responsibility.

JOSH'S STORY: GIVING OTHERS PERMISSION TO STRUGGLE

In 2017, I participated in the Presidential Leadership

Scholars Program. Before attending the first meeting, I was nervous about the people I'd meet in the program. I assumed most of them would be resume-stuffers and elitists. I figured I would hear a lot about what other people did for a living and how great they were.

During our first week of training, I got on a shuttle bus with my fellow participants. Immediately after sitting down, a guy next to me asked what I did. I told him I worked with veterans. He said, "Are you a veteran?" When I told him "no," he asked, "So why do you do this?"

I gave him the whole story—all the pieces I've relayed throughout this book. I shared honestly and matter-of-factly. When I was done, the man just looked at me. Then, he started opening up about when he was depressed. He told me he'd been engaged and then broken off the engagement; he spoke of other struggles he was going through. He had tears streaming down his face. It was like he saw in me a part of himself; he saw in me someone who was capable of honoring his story and his experience.

This happens a lot—basically, as soon as people find out I'm a civilian who works with veterans, I get that first question: "Why?" I've discovered over the years in sharing my story—being honest about the panic attacks, anxiety, and suicidal thoughts—that so many people struggle with the same exact things. Yet often, people don't feel like they have permission to tell anybody. They feel they need to pretend and play the game. But when people hear me openly sharing my dirty laundry without shame or despair—they're inspired. Suddenly, they have the courage to drop their masks too.

Ken and I experience this often at the retreat; as we share, others share too. They trust us and honor us with their stories, knowing that we'll receive them with empathy and compassion. It's an amazing thing to watch people release the weight of their stories and experience the freedom that comes with it. For both of us, this is one of the greatest privileges of being an Expert Guide.

LISTEN WELL

Sharing well is important, but more often, the most helpful way you can serve another person is by simply shutting your mouth and listening. An Expert Guide is somebody who listens well, and who shares from their depths. The listening part is often even more important than the sharing part. The following points identify key practices for listening well. We've compiled these points over the years from various readings and our own experience.[52] We call these points "practices," because they do require practice. Most of us have to work at becoming good listeners. Initially, you might sit there while someone else is sharing and have to be very conscious about staying tuned in.

Your mind wanders. You'll want to touch your phone and have to intentionally stop yourself. But like anything, your listening skills *will* improve as you practice.

BE PRESENT

Good listeners are present and demonstrate their engagement by giving their full, undivided attention. Cell phones are shut off; they move away from their computers. Good listeners do their best to devote sufficient time to the conversation so that the conversation isn't cut off prematurely. Listening well takes time and requires full attention.

MAKE EYE CONTACT

Good listeners look at the person they're listening to and make eye contact. They don't move their lips while "listening," as though they're preparing a response, and they don't roll their eyes. Body language sends a clear message about whether or not you care about what a person says, what you think about it, and how soon you want to respond. Make sure your body language communicates one main message: I care, and I'm interested.

DON'T RESPOND

Good listeners do not respond while somebody else is talking. They don't hum or haw, or hurry up the speaker with statements like, "Oh, yeah, yeah, I understand, I understand." Poor listeners always feel compelled to say something.

Skilled listeners simply listen without forming a response. They might nod their heads, or acknowledge the speaker's statements with a smile, but they don't try to respond. They listen deeply with the goal of hearing what another human being is saying. Period.

DON'T INTERRUPT

When you try to speak honestly, you may talk for a little while and then inevitably, you'll pause. Maybe you're collecting your thoughts, or maybe you're giving the listener an opportunity for judgment. In that pause, the listener chooses to send one of two signals. Either: he interrupts and weighs in with his own ideas; perhaps he tries to finish your sentence, or says, "Oh, that happened to me." Or: the listener signals a desire to hear more by remaining silent. When a person can share without being interrupted, what comes after that first pause is the deep truth, something that rarely gets spoken.

People can be prepped to listen well, in this regard. If the person preparing to share clarifies that she'd like to have the freedom to speak until she explicitly says, "I'm done," a listener has clear expectations established. Alternately, the listener can ask, "Would you like me to ask questions or respond while you're sharing, or would you prefer I just listen until you tell me you're finished?" This also can set up a helpful framework for the conversation. By refraining from interrupting, you allow that person the time and space required to share deeply. Don't try to fill the space; just allow it to sit. The moments that follow those silences are when the truth comes out.

DON'T PARROT

Good listeners don't parrot back a repetition of what an individual has just shared. Parroting another person's words implies that you're not truly attempting to understand the speaker's meaning. Rather, good listeners attempt to clarify and deepen their understanding. They might ask, "Do I understand you? Is this what you mean?"

DON'T FINISH OTHERS' SENTENCES

Good listeners don't try to finish a speaker's sentences. When bad listeners do this, it implies that they already know what the speaker is going to say. If that's the case, then why should the speaker even bother continuing? It sends an invalidating message. As a listener, even if you think you know where the speaker is heading—show them respect by not voicing your "guesses" about where that might be. Just listen and allow them to find their own words in the pauses.

ESTABLISH YOUR ROLE

In a disclosure session, there should be certain expectations about who will be doing most of the sharing, and who will be doing most of the listening. If you're there to be the listener in a conversation, you should listen a lot more than you talk. Consider what percentage you might want to shoot for: perhaps you allow the speaker to do 80 percent of the talking, and you do 20 percent. In casual conversations, you may experience more of a 50/50 relationship in dialogue, but for important times of sharing, clearer roles may need to be established. Some people have the emotional intelligence to naturally sense their roles; other times, a preemptive conversation may be needed where those roles are explicitly identified. "I've got a lot I need to get off my chest—do you mind just listening to me for a while?"

DON'T CHANGE THE TOPIC

Two friends drive in the car together, down a long stretch of freeway. One friend is sharing about his broken marriage with the other and confesses, "When she said that, it hit me...this might be over. I don't know how we're going to survive this." His friend murmurs a distracted acknowledgment, then says excitedly, "Dude! Check out that Ferrari!"

Bad listening. If a person is sharing deeply, a good listener will stay focused. Yes, there might be other things on the listener's mind: the Ferrari, or logistics to be coordinated, or an unrelated question. But practicing good listening requires sticking to the topic at hand. Let the person sharing decide when it's time to shift gears. A good listener stays focused and attentive on the story being shared, even if distractions are present.

ASK OPEN-ENDED QUESTIONS (DON'T GIVE ADVICE)

These last two points are, in our opinion, the most important elements of good listening, so we'll spend more time discussing them.

Let's imagine that you're struggling, and you want to talk about your problems with someone. You choose a trusted confidant and spill your guts. You were hoping they'd just listen; instead, as soon as you finish your thought, the listener jumps in: "I know how you need to fix this..." The listener proceeds to give you all kinds of advice about what you should do. You sense your friend is trying to be helpful.

(It's not helpful.)

When you try to solve someone's problems or tell that person what to do, you send a clear message: "I don't think you're capable of solving this on your own." Unfortunately, rather than building a deeper connection in a relationship, this type of bad listening—offering advice—sets up a relationship of inequality. The listener is trying to *control* the person struggling, rather than attempting to connect on the same level and understand.

Every human being has a deep need to be heard, to be seen, and to be validated. You can't accomplish any of that as a listener if you treat the person sharing as though he or she is incapable. Unsolicited advice, essentially, is criticism. It's an indication that you don't think the person struggling has the ideas, the wherewithal, or the capability to solve his problems.

But then what is the listener supposed to do, after hearing a friend spout off all kinds of problems that need fixing? Two types of responses will be far more helpful than offering advice. One: ask open-ended questions to help your friend come to his or her own conclusions. Two: share your experience of what's been helpful for you, without converting it to advice about what will work for someone else.

Asking open-ended questions helps people think deeply about their struggle and arrive at their own decisions.

Rather than trying to drive someone into a decision-making process, a good listener supports another human being getting to where she wants to go on her own terms, in a way that honors her dignity. At the end of the day, most people know what's right and what's wrong. They even often know what to do—though they might not yet understand what inhibits them from doing it. Sometimes people just need to dig a little bit deeper to find that answer within. A good friend, with good questions, can help someone find those answers.

Secondly, share your experience, rather than advice. It's important to understand in any conversation that your perception is "X"—based on your own experiences. Someone else is going to be entering the conversation with an entirely different set of experiences, and will have different perceptions as a result. If you start to give advice from "X," you start to run others down a road that's not necessarily true for them.

What you *can* do is share the experiences that you have in common, and allow your friends to form their own conclusions about what might be a helpful next step. Either before or after you share about your own experience, ask those open-ended questions to help them process what they might need to do.

KEN'S STORY: ASKING OPEN-ENDED QUESTIONS AND SHARING EXPERIENCE

On one of my tours of duty, I had a guy that worked for me. Some days he'd come into work with a black eye, and he often looked miserable. I learned that he and his wife were very physical with each other, and his wife was as big as he was. She sometimes punched him, and her kids would join her; his stepson stabbed him once. It was clearly an abusive relationship.

I may have thought to myself, "This guy is crazy. Why is he living in that house? Why wouldn't he just leave?"— but I didn't say that. I wanted him to get to that point on his own. One day I just said to him, "Do you really love her?"

He looked at me and said, "I'm not sure."

I asked, "Well, what will it take for you to be sure?" He paused and thought about that. I said, "Do you enjoy coming to work like this? You're late. I'm getting calls from the police station because you've been stabbed, or because your son's driving an illegal car around the base. I'm getting phone calls from your neighbors who are complaining. So what is it going to take for you to understand whether or not you love her?" Those types of questions opened up a dialogue that forced the guy to go deep and think about what was going on in his life.

There have been times when people came to me specifically asking for advice, but even then, I think it's better to share experiences and ask questions. I was a speaker at a big bomb disposal event in Washington DC, and talked about my first company, A-T Solutions. After my presentation, a guy approached me and said, "My company is really struggling. How the hell did you do it?"

I said to him, "I'd be happy to sit down and talk to you about your struggle, but you can't compare your company to mine. I launched my company just before the Iraq war, when we had hundreds of thousands of troops training and deploying to war. But the wars are winding down and so are the service-related contracts." I told him, "I'd like to think I'm a decent leader, but a lot of our success had to do with having the right product at the right time. If you'd like though, I'd be happy to sit down with you and go through your company's stats and look at your business development strategy." We were set to start the conversation from there.

I easily could have said, "You should do what I do." But that's the easy way out, and in the long run, it wouldn't have helped this guy much. Whether a conversation occurs over something as superficial as buying a Chevy versus a Ford, or as deep as a struggling marriage, sharing experiences and asking questions is going to be far more helpful than offering advice.

One last word of caution: be especially skeptical of advice that comes from anyone whose life is incongruent. If you're seeking out financial help, and your banker's own finances are a train wreck—in no way should that person be handing out advice about money. This extends to you too. If a friend comes to you because they're struggling to get physically fit, and you know your own physical category in the Wellness Triangle is at a "two"—don't give them advice. You're not equipped to guide someone in an area where you are not congruent. Even after achieving congruence, you will still be a more helpful guide to those coming to you for help if you simply share your own experience and ask good questions.

SHOW EMPATHY

The last and most important element of good listening is showing empathy. An empathetic listener witnesses without judgment and shows a willingness to share another person's burden. If you take a rock out of your rucksack and hand it off to someone empathetic, that person will make you feel safe, will be trustworthy, and will ultimately help you put that rock down.

Empathetic listeners show that they hold you in positive regard. They don't question your intentions or make assumptions. Rather, they believe in your intentions and in the relationship. When you can be sure that another person values you, and will continue to value you, it becomes possible to be honest about nearly anything.

Don't underestimate the profound impact you might be able to have on someone struggling through empathetic listening. Research shows that for the vast majority of people, empathetic listening produces substantial gains in mental health.[53] One experiment called the "Friendship Bench Project" has been conducted in Zimbabwe, where grandmothers are available to listen to anyone who might need to share.[54] An estimated 27,000 people have been helped and counseled by these trained but non-expert grandmothers. These women offer their time and willingness to listen to others with empathy; for literally thousands of struggling people, that help is enough to regain strength to move forward.

There's also no hierarchy in a relationship defined by empathy. Sympathy is different; sympathetic people feel a sense of pity for those struggling. They look down at someone: "You poor thing." In contrast, empathy means you put yourself in a struggling person's shoes. Whereas the sympathetic person looks down at someone as "the other," the empathetic person communicates, "I'm the same as you."

How do you teach empathy or learn to be empathetic? This might be the toughest skill to both teach and learn.

Much of the learning process starts with following these first nine steps of becoming a good listener. Once you hone good listening skills, showing other people that you genuinely care about what they have to say, empathy naturally starts to appear.

Empathy is also learned by going through your own journey from struggle to strength, and choosing to risk disclosure. The "inside-out" strategy requires you to look deep inside yourself, acknowledge the gifts and pain you carry, and then offer up your story to others. An "outside-in" person—someone who lives with the head and heart disconnected, functioning from a place of ego—is going to have a hard time showing empathy. You can't show deep compassion if you're someone who survives by functioning only at a surface level.

But those who have connected their heads and hearts understand the struggle we're all dealing with. As you walk through this process yourself, empathy becomes the natural outcome of a person who is connected, who is whole, who is struggling well. You're also more equipped to show compassion, rather than judgment. For instance, let's say that a coworker is frustrating you. If you've gone through the long process of getting on top of your own struggle, you're not going to beat up someone else for being in a bad place. You're going to understand where they are and forgive them for what they're doing. You'll have the capacity to connect with that person and ask what's going on.

"People will forget what you did, and they'll forget what you said, but they'll never forget how you made them feel."[55]

—CARL BUEHNER

JOSH'S STORY: THE GIFT OF EMPATHY

I remember the experience of calling up my friends to tell them that I was getting divorced. I anxiously geared up to share the news with one of my best friends whom I'd known since I was fourteen. He was married and religious—I was worried that he was going to be judgmental.

I called him and said, "Hey, Rashad, I'm getting divorced." He first responded by saying he was sorry to hear that, and asked me how I was doing. Then he said, "I know one thing for sure. The only people who know what happens in a relationship are the two people in it. Those are the only two people entitled to an opinion about what the right decision is. I just want to make sure that you're okay. I'm here if you need me."

That, to me, was empathy. Rashad knew what he knew and what he didn't know, and he communicated that in a way that honored the place I was at. Examples like his, and traveling my own road from struggle to strength, have taught me how to show others I'm safe to confide in.

PREPARING TO BE AN EXPERT GUIDE

You've summited Mount Struggle, and you're ready to lead others up the same path. As you prepare for leadership, take yourself through a mental inventory and ensure you have what you need.

Check your Wellness Triangle. Are you ready to lead? Your categories may not all be fives yet, but they should be equally balanced, strong, and heading in the right direction guided by a clear set of goals. You understand what happens if you backslide, and how to rally without having to endure another self-inflicted disaster. You understand that you've got a new positive story to share with others, and can share your past story with self-mastery, without reliving it.

Check your head and your heart. Are you ready to lead? You should be able to access your deepest-held emotions, values, and beliefs, in a way that gives you clear direction and purpose for your future. Your decisions and strategies are informed by the values you've determined to be true for you. You are connected with yourself and experience greater ease in connecting with others.

This connectedness is crucial. Remember that the limiting factor to your ability to help others is your capacity to connect with yourself. You can't save someone from drowning if you don't know how to swim, and similarly, you won't be able to connect with others if you can't connect with yourself.

If you attempt to help others before doing the hard work of connecting your own head and heart, your "help" will end up looking more like manipulation. Lacking self-awareness, this puts you in a place where you're trying to control somebody else or give them advice. Remember, the manner in which you live your life is far more important than anything you say or do; that's why we so strongly recommend ensuring your own strength and health first.

And what will distinguish someone who is living in a manner that others recognize as strong, healthy, and fulfilled? Congruence.

Therefore, check your congruence as well. Are you ready to lead? Your thoughts, your feelings, and actions should all be aligned. You practice what you preach. You're not infallible—you're not Jesus—but as consistently as possible, you live according to your principles and would not be accused of hypocrisy. You do what you say you're going to do, and people know they can trust you.

HOW DO YOU BECOME AN EXPERT GUIDE?

"Expert Guide" is not something you put on your business card. You can't apply for a certificate to hang on your wall, and you shouldn't start knocking on doors, offering to help people address their dysfunction through your "Expert Guidance!"

Being an Expert Guide is more about a lifestyle change—a change that makes you stand out as someone others can trust and turn to for support. In many ways, the training we offer trains people to be better friends. The recommendations we've outlined for being an Expert Guide describe what you should do in any situation.

You should listen more than you talk. You should ask questions to ensure you're not making assumptions, and in doing so, help lead people to their own conclusions. You should share your experiences and hold back from giving advice. Have the capacity to be with another human being, without trying to alter or change them—without trying to tell them what to do. Just be with them; wherever they are is where you are. In all your interactions, bring a listening ear, authenticity, and empathy for others. The role of Expert Guide describes a way of *being*, more than a job title.

Living in such a way draws other people to you. They'll wonder why you're different, why you are the way you are, and how you got there. Because of the changed perspective you've achieved in your own journey through struggle, you'll be that much more tuned into people who need help. And as those conversations begin, you'll be stepping into the role of Expert Guide.

This is not a moment for fanfare; you're not trying to accumulate clients. This is a moment for humility. Keep in mind the idea that the best relationships are mutually beneficial. Even in relationships where you're the "teacher," you're still always the student—as you guide others, they'll be able to teach you. In the process, you'll experience the deep human connection that comes within a reciprocal relationship. Your ultimate goal? Live in a manner that helps improve your life and the lives of everybody around you, without desiring credit for doing so.

KEN'S STORY: TRAINING FOR LIFE

Perhaps this Expert Guide chapter seems intimidating, but it all comes back to the importance of training. My work dismantling explosives in the military shocks people when they hear about it. People ask me, "How'd you avoid getting blown up?" I always tell them it comes down to the fact that I was trained properly. Without proper training, no one would ever think to approach a land mine or try to cut a trip wire. But with training, it becomes a practical and straightforward thing to do.

Likewise, our goal with this book is train you how to struggle well. We're trying to train you to get through the minefield of life and enable others to follow behind you. Good training allows you to overcome tasks that initially appear daunting, without making mistakes. When dismantling a bomb, there's no room for error—and life doesn't offer many second chances either. If you don't train bomb disposal specialists properly, and more importantly if those specialists don't put the training to use and instead decide to shortcut operations, bad things happen. We want to emphasize the same attention to detail here. None of us are getting out alive. The time to start living well is now.

Remember that, in some ways, you've already experienced a lifetime of training. Yes, your past experiences left you with some challenges to sort through, but don't forget about the gifts you took from them as well. The years I spent beside my mom's bedside while she went through cancer trained me to sit beside the hospital beds of EOD guys who had suffered terrible injuries. Although I wasn't yet working with the term, "Expert Guide," those were some of my first real "expert guiding" moments. I sat with these guys and listened to their stories in a way that tried to honor their dignity. I didn't offer advice; I just tried to be an empathetic friend.

If you've read this book and done the work, then you've

completed most of the training you need on the journey of Posttraumatic Growth. You now have the opportunity to use your training to offer others what you have experienced. And that's the deal—this is non-negotiable: if you climb to the top of the mountain, you come back down and you help other people up.

EMBRACING THE CALL

The pinnacle of Posttraumatic Growth isn't reaching the summit of Mount Struggle; it's your decision to go back down and help others make the ascent. Maybe you didn't complete each step of the journey in the order that we outlined in the book; this path is rarely, if ever, mechanistic. It looks different for everyone. But if you've completed the phases of PTG, your next step will be guiding others up this mountain. That's the epitome of Posttraumatic Growth.

Being an Expert Guide means that when you encounter people, you make yourself available to listen and are honest about your own story. You show others that they can be authentic with you and trust another human being. Through sharing your experience, you demonstrate that others can also be open to a new life and new possibilities.

"The meaning of your life is to help others find the meaning of theirs."[56]

—VIKTOR FRANKL, *MAN'S SEARCH FOR MEANING*

One of the major incentives of getting well isn't just to feel better—it's so that you can *do* better. You can serve as a guide, leading people out of the darkness and into a great life. As an Expert Guide, you're given the opportunity to get well for a purpose, as if getting well weren't reason enough on its own.

At every moment of every day, you encounter people carrying burdens—carrying stories. You have an opportunity to alter the fate of someone else's life by the way you engage them and make them feel. You can alter everything they think is possible for their existence. Can you imagine a greater privilege?

You don't do it for the glory, you don't do it for the money; you do it because it's what you needed when you struggled, and it's what other people deserve.

CONCLUSION

—

"Live your life that the fear of death can never enter your heart. Trouble no one about their religion, respect others and their view, and demand that they respect yours. Love your life. Perfect your life. Beautify all things in your life. Seek to make your life long and its purpose in the service of your people. When it comes your time to die, be not like those whose hearts are filled with the fear of death so that when their time comes they weep and pray for a little more time to live their lives over again in a different way. Sing your death song and die like a hero going home."[57]

—TECUMSEH

Tecumseh, the man who spoke the words above, is one of the most celebrated Indian Chiefs in history. Not only did he manage to rally together many disparate tribes into a unified force, he was known for his ambition and his eloquence. He took risks and made selfless sacrifices for the survival of his people; he lived his life boldly for others and never looked back. For these reasons and others, his statue stands at the US Naval Academy. The quote above is included with the statue, reminding all who gaze upon it to live well, to live for others, to live bravely.

These words should compel us. They identify a credo for how to live a life you can feel proud of, one that is mindful of the legacy you'll leave behind. Tecumseh expected his people to take care of themselves and live lives of service. He fought for his beliefs to the end of his life when he was killed in battle, and he reminds us to live without fear.

And what should you fear? You have the choice—even in the moments when you feel closest to death—to act "like a hero going home." In our terms, heroes are ordinary people who survive an extraordinary experience, and return to share important truths about life that they learned so they can enrich the lives of others. You survived the worst; you are tested and transformed; you share the lessons you learned with others—that is what we call a Hero.

You may have read this book because you're struggling, or you care about someone who struggles. If that's the case, then you are not alone; this well-worn road is the rule, not the exception. Although people often refrain from acknowledging their burdens, we are at our most human when we struggle. It's what unites us as humans; we all go through painful and joyful moments.

Struggle exposes your soul, liberating you to be who you truly are and allowing you to abandon the pretense of who you were pretending to be. In that way, struggle can usher in profound beauty. Once you acknowledge the gifts struggle can offer you, you take the first step out of that mental prison Charlie Plumb identified in our book's Foreword. Struggle forces you to reset your priorities, re-examine your beliefs about yourself and the world, and develop the kind of sustainable authenticity that will enable you to serve the people you love.

When you're in the middle of the hardest experience of your life, it's difficult to see what "gifts" a tragedy could possibly hold; it's hard to see anything beyond the pain. We get that. But remember that there is a next day coming; eventually, there will be an "after." You will be different in the "after"—and it's likely that you'll encounter others who need to hear your story, once you're there.

Every struggle you endure builds up your strength. You have the choice to make new decisions, ones that better equip you to endure every challenge from here on out. Our experiences in helping thousands of men and women overcome struggle shows us that "the after" can be filled with joy, service, purpose, and deep fulfillment.

KEN'S STORY: THE SIGN OF THE STRONGEST

Right before I got out of the Navy, I was on a task force that worked to integrate Navy bomb disposal personnel into every deploying SEAL Team. Initially, it was a challenge to find the guys who would be most successful; not everybody's cut out to integrate with Navy SEALs. One SEAL advised me on how we could weed out the strongest from those who wouldn't cut it; he shared with me three categories of identification.

The first category of Sailor they identified was the ultimate athlete—the top high school swimmer, the star quarterback. Ironically though, these ultimate athletes usually weren't able to cut the SEAL training. In their past, nobody had ever slapped them around. As soon as somebody was yelling in the ultimate athlete's face, that candidate would likely drop out.

A second category described the guy that could barely make it through high school. Maybe he played football, but only every other season because his grades weren't great. As with the ultimate athletes, this category of Sailor usually couldn't cut it either. They hadn't developed the discipline needed to keep up, and were up and down too much of the time.

The third category described the strongest Sailors—the ones who would be able to make the team. These were the

Sailors who ran in the middle of the pack; they'd passed the physical screening by working like hell. These were the backup quarterbacks instead of the lead quarterbacks; these were the number two swimmers. These were the guys who'd had to work for every accomplishment, and they knew the road from struggle to strength, well. Those are the warriors we can count on to go the distance.

Struggle brings pain; it's undeniable. But it changes you in ways that nothing else can. For that reason, we believe it offers some of the best gifts you will ever encounter—IF you choose to embrace them.

POINTS TO REMEMBER
STRUGGLE IS OUR HISTORY

From Buddha to Jesus, from Auschwitz to the Hanoi Hilton, the stories of people who endured the most unfathomable suffering are the ones who bring wisdom to the rest of us. It's easy to get stuck in a rut of habit; you go through the motions of your life and don't stop to question those habits until a crisis hits. It's when you get a shock to the system—cancer, a divorce, death of a loved one, injury, job loss—that you start making changes.

Some of the wellness practices that people turn to in those moments are practices that have sustained people through struggle for thousands of years, like yoga, meditation, or prayer. In forming new habits that incorporate wellness practices, you'll find that the habits that help you through struggle are the same practices that also keep you healthy, successful, and purposeful.

History has produced countless stories of wisdom that came from struggle, along with time-tested wellness practices; both of these can help and guide you. Remember also the history of struggle within your three-to-five network. These people each have their own lifetime of experiences and have likely accumulated wisdom—just as you are through your struggle—that can help you along your way. Seek out people who have experiences worth hearing, and be wary of those who simply offer advice.

IT ALL STARTS WITH YOU

Struggle comes to everyone, but not everyone learns to struggle well. If you want to be someone who manages to get out of the React Sine Wave of reactions, bad habits, and generational trauma—you have to take action. You are the one responsible for learning how to self-regulate. You are the one who must examine your past to achieve freedom and understanding. You are the only one who can create a powerful support network around yourself.

Life is hard work. Struggle tends to shatter our confidence. Admittedly, it's hard to motivate yourself to do the hard work and get back on your feet after repeatedly getting knocked down. When you don't believe in yourself and have little faith in the world, it's challenging to muster the energy to make the major changes required for a new life.

And yet—nobody can do this for you. It *does* require hard work. A support network helps. The wisdom of your elders and in books helps. But in the end, 99 percent of whether or not it works, is up to you.

We met a taxi driver recently from South Sudan, and when we asked how things were going in his country, he said, "They're terrible." He explained the conflicts and the enormous challenges people in his country were facing. Then he said, "But I got out of there, and I'm here now. I'm making enough money that I can send for my wife and child. They're coming over here next month."

Struggle looks different for everyone; the size of the challenge is relative for each individual. But this taxi driver exemplifies the fact that there are always choices you can make and actions you can take to change your situation. In some contexts, those choices are limited—but they're still there. You can still choose to be a person of integrity and of values, regardless of your circumstances.

No matter what kind of struggle is thrown at you, there's going to be some element that requires hard work if you hope to move beyond it. If you don't do the work, then you become the victim, because the question ends up becoming, "Why me?"

The destructive coping mechanisms are easy. It's easy to stay on the couch watching Netflix, and to pop the lid off another beer. It's easier to scroll through Facebook than call someone up you respect and schedule lunch. These lazy coping mechanisms don't get you anywhere though; in fact, inactivity, drinking, and hours in front of a screen are more likely to suck you deeper into struggle than help you move beyond it. You have to work on cultivating your own sense of wellness and connection, sharpening the outside of your Wellness Triangle and inflating that spirituality ball in the inside of your Wellness Triangle.

Taking these steps even when you feel totally depleted requires an ethic familiar to people who've been in the military—just when you think you have nothing left to give, you must keep going and give more. By and large, combat veterans refuse to give others the opportunity to either walk around their issues or to be overwhelmed by them. They believe challenges need to be confronted head-on, and we need to find the courage and strength to walk through them. Walking through the fire is the point of life. If you don't push yourself to struggle well and live well, you're going to find yourself on your deathbed wishing you had lived differently.

One of the things that we most admire about men and women who have been in combat is that they have a "PhD in GSD," which is "Getting Shit Done." They are people of action. They measure themselves and others by whether or not they do what they said they're going to do. As you've read this book and explored these ideas, you've spent time reflecting. Now it is time to go apply these ideas. It is time to be a person of integrity, a person who does what they say they are going to do. It is time to begin to walk that road from struggle to strength.

POSTTRAUMATIC GROWTH: THE REAL GIFT

What you gain along the journey from struggle to strength is clearly spelled out in the domains of Posttraumatic Growth. You achieve **deeper relationships** with other people; you're able to let people into your life in deep and meaningful ways and support others through profound levels of connectedness.

You find a sense of **personal strength** that you never thought you possessed. You know that you can wake up and deal with anything, and this new confidence acts as fuel to help you become a stronger and better person.

You gain a profound **appreciation for life**. You're grateful for the basic gifts of being able to wake up, of having some semblance of your health, and of being able to connect with other people that matter and you care about.

You recognize **new possibilities**, even while you develop more realistic expectations about what life will bring you. Struggle is guaranteed, but you feel less limited and more hopeful about where the world might take you.

Lastly, you gain a greater sense of the **meaning** of life and death, and know what life is really about. Those are the gifts you acquire while you walk that road from struggle to strength. Other than reading about these treasures in books, you can really only acquire these treasures internally—on a "soul" level—through struggle. If there's one purpose of struggle, it's to help you have a clear-eyed view of what genuinely matters in your life.

FOUR KEYS TO LIVING WELL

We've written extensively on struggling well, and we also want to emphasize that many of these same concepts are also the key to living well. Once the struggle passes, and you've done the hard work to struggle well—how do you maintain your forward momentum? How do you work to stay away from the volatile React Sine Wave, and keep yourself in the Response Sine Wave?

There are four keys to living well—to achieving meaning and purpose in your life:

1. Review your past experiences: understand them, integrate them, and occasionally review and share them.
2. Cultivate wellness practices in the areas of mind, body, finance, and spirit.
3. Build meaningful relationships by staying connected to a close network of three to five healthy people.
4. Carry out acts of service to others.

REVIEW YOUR PAST EXPERIENCES

Remember the red Ferrari? Early in the book we had you imagine driving off a lot in your dream car—and then inching along the road at ten miles per hour, because you couldn't take your eyes off the rearview mirror to drive the road in front of you. That's a picture of how living in the past robs you of the kind of rich experiences you could enjoy, if you only freed yourself from the hold of past trauma. You just can't get through life staring in the rearview mirror, but to be a great driver, you've still got to understand what's back there.

You find that freedom and understanding by examining your past, and then disclosing it to trusted, empathetic listeners. By completing an exercise like "My Old Story," you create a body of experience that you can reference for both its gifts and its challenges. There's the understanding; you begin to recognize that meaning and strength emerged from even your worst times. The M.O.S. exercise also helps you consider more deeply what the people in your story may have been dealing with and develop compassion for them. This can help you arrive at compassion for yourself as well, which will be strengthened through disclosing your story to empathetic listeners. There's the freedom.

Once you understand your past experiences, then it's important to integrate those lessons into your life moving forward. Make changes in your life that prevent you from repeating the same mistakes. Pursue new opportunities with a better understanding about how your past experiences helped further your story, gifts, and abilities. Share your experiences with others that are coming through struggle.

We used to have a buddy who would say, "Those ten years of my life are black, and I don't ever want to talk or think about them." But his words were counterproductive; clearly, those ten years still had a severe impact on him today. If you adopt the same attitude, you'll remain stuck. Instead, get yourself to a place where you can say, "Yes, these things happened. I can look at them, and I'm not afraid of my story or my experiences. I can understand how even the most horrific experiences can serve as teachers for me."

Facing your past in such a way can even lead you to purposeful work in the future, perhaps through working with people who have similar experiences, or by working to prevent your life's traumas from happening to others. Each new struggle teaches you more fully about who you are, provided you mine your experiences for what they can teach you, so you don't continue to make the same mistakes.

HAVE WELLNESS PRACTICES AND LEAN INTO YOUR SUPPORT NETWORK

Once you've got your eyes on the road in front of you, and you've got that Ferrari up to a healthy cruising speed, you need to drive well by staying within the boundary lines. The boundaries to keep you living well are ones we've hit time and again in this book: wellness practices, and your network of three-to-five people. Those two components are the keys to maintaining a sense of calm and clarity when life slaps you in the face. They help you avoid negatively reacting in ways that launch you into the unstable cycle of the React Sine Wave.

After making peace with your past experiences, continue to build on your wellness practices to the point where you're learning different things, you're mastering them, and you're teaching them to others. Work on each category of your Wellness Triangle, always seeking to sharpen the edges and inflate the ball in the middle. Also, build your support network, and be part of other people's positive three to five. Surround yourself with people who can see through your "Instagram filters" and will insist on you being honest. Turn to these people for accountability and support as you pursue a better life.

SERVE OTHERS

Finally, always engage in service in different ways, forms, and degrees. You can start by simply telling your story. The ultimate outcome for your PTG journey is helping others through their own journeys by sharing your experiences in a helpful way.

Remember the eulogy you're creating while you live. You're not here for yourself. The reason people admire others is because they made a positive impact on the world. After you're gone, you will be measured by the impact and influence you had on other people. It's not about you; it's about taking care of yourself and your responsibilities so that you can serve other humans. Ironically, in serving others over yourself, you'll become more happy, fulfilled, and purposeful. It's a beautiful, virtuous cycle.

LIVE HEROICALLY

Five days before Charlie Plumb was scheduled to come home from war, he was shot down and ended up spending six years as a POW in "The Hanoi Hilton." Like every other prisoner of war, he had violated the military's code of conduct, because during torture, he had broken. Although he didn't have many secrets to begin with, he still felt deep shame until a fellow prisoner told him, "It's okay. Everybody broke. There isn't a man in this camp who was as strong as he wanted to be." The leadership in these camps helped normalize the struggles and failures of everyone in the camp, creating for their Soldiers the trusted network of support that enabled them to endure unbelievable horrors.

When Charlie came home from war, he still had broken bones. He had abscesses. He had infections in his body. On top of it all, he found out his wife had left him, because she thought he was dead. His struggle didn't end when he left the Hanoi Hilton; in some ways, it worsened. Then Charlie remembered the lessons of his experiences and regained the faith to know he would get through his struggle. He had spent six years perfecting the ability to self-regulate himself amongst the worst that humanity had to offer. He built a new support network and chose to create hope, meaning, and purpose in his life.

During World War II, Viktor Frankl was taken prisoner, along with millions of other Jews, and was forced to work in a concentration camp. Although he was treated like every other prisoner in the camp, because of his experience as a doctor, he had the opportunity to help others in the camp. After enduring starvation, sickness, brutality, humiliation, and witnessing his fellow men give wholly into despair, Frankl was still called upon to serve others—in spite of his own pain. As a doctor, he cared for sick prisoners in the camp. Even more powerfully, he was asked one night to give a message of hope to other prisoners, forcing him to rise above his own misery for the sake of others.

Like Charlie, Frankl endured many of his worst experiences by nurturing the hope of seeing his wife again. After the Allies liberated him from the camp, he learned that his wife had died just after her own camp's liberation, from starvation. The last indignity wasn't the concentration camp. And yet, like Charlie, the trauma Frankl endured didn't define how he was going to live the rest of his life.

Both of these men went on to live lives that inspire and encourage others. Although they experienced arguably the worst that humanity has to offer, they each learned to embrace their struggle for meaning. They shared their stories so that others could thrive. Frankl and Plumb's vision is to offer a message of encouragement so that others have the strength to endure times of suffering with hope. Frankl lived, and Charlie continues to live, honorable, service-oriented lives, choosing to be the heroes of their own journeys.

Like Plumb and Frankl, you have to live and be strong *because* of your experiences, not in spite of them. Viktor Frankl was Viktor Frankl because of his time in Auschwitz, and Charlie Plumb because of his time in the Hanoi Hilton. Those tests forged these men and made them the heroes that they are.

Struggle is the story of every great leader, every great man, and every great woman. Through encountering obstacles, heroes are tested and forged into becoming the great, authentic human beings they are destined to be.

Your birthright is to go through the crucible and be forged in the fire. It's your birthright to return from struggle without resentment or hostility, but with the goal of serving others. It's your birthright to rise from the ashes with a sense of honor and integrity that allows you to be a leader in your own life, and the lives of your family, community, and country.

Within you lies the ability to summon the courage and power that's required to travel the road from struggle to strength. We hope this book provides some of the guidance needed for your journey, and the hope to recognize that tomorrow doesn't have to be anything like yesterday. Your worst yesterdays can in fact make for amazing tomorrows.

"It matters not how strait the gate, how charged with punishments the scroll.

I am the master of my fate. I am the captain of my soul."[58]

—ERNEST HENLEY, "INVICTUS"

You've read the book; now go *do* the book. You have a choice to recognize struggle as an opportunity. You have the choice to become the hero in your own story. You have the choice to live in such a way that you are able to serve others from a place of fulfillment, strength, and joy.

Life is a choice. Be the master of your fate. Be the captain of your soul. Struggle Well.

ACKNOWLEDGMENTS

KEN FALKE

This book is dedicated to the men and women of the military who serve our nation so selflessly. Your service transcends the selfishness of our world. Come home from war and be the productive members of society here that you were there. Our nation needs you and your leadership to help others learn how to struggle well!

You can't write a book these days, hold a job, raise a family, and run three businesses without sacrificing something. First, I would like to thank my wife for her patience with my absence while I was deployed during my military service, on the road for business, on the phone, or behind a computer screen. Thank you, Julia; you are the rock of our family and the love of my life. To my beautiful daughters, Gennavieve and Rhian, my son-in-law, Brayden, and my four grandkids, Troy, Riley, Cameron, and Gwendolyn, thank you. I will never get the time away from you back, and I hope to spend more time with you as I grow old.

To Captain Charlie Plumb, you are an inspiration to all humans to master "struggling well." And to Dr. Rich Tedeschi and Dr. Bret Moore, thank you for putting the science behind our success and believing in our work at Boulder Crest.

To Mr. Bernie Marcus and the Marcus Foundation staff for believing in us and making a leadership investment that allowed us to develop a solution to these challenges that is both transformative and scalable.

To the US Navy EOD community and all my friends, you are my second family! To my third family, A-T Solutions, the EOD Warrior Foundation, and Boulder Crest, I am very grateful to you as my teammates for all you do to make other lives and our lives a success.

To my stepmother, Maureen, you filled a hole in my life that I never thought could be full again. I know I wasn't an easy kid, but you never showed me anything but love. Thank you.

And finally, to my dad. Your words of wisdom shaped my life. You made me the man I am and I'll spend the rest of my life translating and sharing the lessons I learned from you. You are sorely missed, and I am grateful to live your legacy!

JOSH GOLDBERG

I am alive, fulfilled, and purposeful because of the kindness, wisdom, and mentorship of some incredibly special human beings. As a broad class, that begins with combat veterans, who taught me the meaning of strength, community, integrity, and service. To them, I will remain forever indebted and committed to paying it forward in each and every circumstance.

To Mort, Todd, Ken, Dusty, Suzi, Dustin, Roman, Michael, Seb, Norman, Grandma, and the many other teachers who crossed my path when I was ready and able to listen, thank you. You have made an indelible mark on my soul, and made me the man I am today. To Viktor Frankl, Joseph Campbell, and James Stockdale, thanks for laying the tracks.

To my parents, thank you for the incredible foundation you provided and your enduring support. To my brother, Jeremy, thank you for pushing and challenging me to make the most of my talents. To my sister-in-law, Jenna, thanks for that walkabout suggestion. To my niece, Ever, and my nephew, Oz, thank you for showing me the meaning of love and connection, and how important it is to remain curious about life.

To my teammates across the Boulder Crest and PATHH worlds, thank you for your inspiration, passion, and commitment. It is beyond a joy to walk this road with you.

Lastly—to you, the reader—we acknowledge your strength, persistence, perseverance, and commitment to living a meaningful and fulfilling life. Just know that it is out there, and it is worth the struggle. Struggle Well!

ABOUT THE
AUTHORS

———

KEN FALKE spent 21 years in the US Navy as a bomb disposal specialist. After retiring from the Navy in 2002, Ken started and later sold A-T Solutions, a counter-terrorism company. In 2007, Ken founded the EOD Warrior Foundation to support the families of severely wounded military bomb disposal personnel. This work inspired Ken and his family to donate 37 acres of their estate in Bluemont, Virginia and millions of dollars to build Boulder Crest Retreat Virginia in 2013—the nation's first privately funded wellness center dedicated exclusively to combat veterans and their families—and go on to establish Boulder Crest Retreat Arizona and the Boulder Crest Institute in 2017.

JOSH GOLDBERG is the Executive Director of the Boulder Crest Institute, which is dedicated to the advancement and application of the science of Posttraumatic Growth.

After spending 11 years as a communications executive for two of the world's biggest corporations, Josh's world came crashing down, as he grappled with severe anxiety, depression, and thoughts of suicide. Although Josh initially sought to get well by helping others, the veterans he was "helping" ended up saving his life. Their strength, integrity, and brotherhood helped Josh develop a deep and abiding sense of strength, and a new tribe. In 2013, Josh met Ken Falke, and soon after joined the staff of Boulder Crest. He ultimately led the development of Warrior PATHH, the nation's first-ever program designed to cultivate and facilitate Posttraumatic Growth amongst combat veterans. In 2018, Josh and Ken co-founded the Boulder Crest Institute, which seeks to help all those who struggle walk the road from struggle to profound strength and lifelong growth.

REFERENCES

1 Statistic obtained by the EOD Warrior Foundation. Contact eodwarriorfoundation. org for more information.

2 Statistic obtained by the EOD Warrior Foundation. Contact eodwarriorfoundation. org for more information.

3 Tanielian, Terri, Coreen Farris, Caroline Batka, Carrie M. Farmer, Eric Robinson, Charles C. Engel, Michael Robbins and Lisa H. Jaycox. Ready to Serve: Community-Based Provider Capacity to Deliver Culturally Competent, Quality Mental Health Care to Veterans and Their Families. Santa Monica, CA: RAND Corporation, 2014. https://www.rand.org/pubs/research_reports/RR806.html.

4 Tedeschi, R.G., & Calhoun, L.G. (1995). *Trauma and Transformation: Growing in the Aftermath of Suffering*. Thousand Oaks, CA: Sage.

5 Campbell, Joseph, Bill D. Moyers, and Betty S. Flowers. *The Power of Myth*. Turtleback Books, 2012.

6 Schopenhauer, Arthur. *Studies in Pessimism*. Whitefish, MT: Kessinger Publishing, 2008.

7 Hill, Napoleon. *Think and Grow Rich*. PA: Sound Wisdom, 1937.

8 Kierkegaard, Soren; tr. by Alexander Dru. *The Journals of Kierkegaard*. 2nd ed. New York: Harper & Row, 1959.

9 Stevens, Jane Ellen. "Addiction Doc says: It's Not the Drugs. It's the ACEs...Adverse Childhood Experiences." ACEs Too High. May 02, 2017. Accessed November 03, 2017. https://acestoohigh.com/2017/05/02/ addiction-doc-says-stop-chasing-the-drug-focus-on-aces-people-can-recover/.

10 Associated Press. "Childhood Traumas More Common in Military Members." Sandiegouniontribune.com. July 23, 2014. Accessed September 11, 2017. http://www.sandiegouniontribune.com/sdut-childhood-traumas-more-common-in-military-members-2014jul23-story.html.

11 Griffith, James, and Craig J. Bryan. "Trauma Before Enlistment Linked to High Suicide Rates Among Military Personnel, Veterans, Research Finds." American Psychological Association. August 9, 2014. Accessed September 11, 2017. http://www.apa.org/news/press/releases/2014/08/military-suicide.aspx.

12 Bethell, Christina PhD, MBA, MPH. "Prioritizing Possibilities for Community Health and Well-Being; The Problem of Adverse Childhood Experiences and the Promise of Prevention, Resilience, and Healing." PowerPoint lecture from Johns Hopkins Bloomberg School of Public Health, Child and Adolescent Health Measurement Initiative, Baltimore, February 2017.

13 Katon, Jodie G., et al. "Adverse Childhood Experiences, Military Trauma, and Adult Health." American Journal of Preventative Medicine 49, no. 4 (October 2015): 573-82. http://www.ajpmonline.org/article/S0749-3797(15)00142-7/fulltext.

14 Jung, Carl Gustav. Visions: Notes of the Seminar Given in 1930-1934 by C.G. Jung. Vol. 1. Princeton University Press, 1997.

15 Brown, Brené. Daring Greatly: How the Courage to be Vulnerable Transforms the Way We Live, Love, Parent, and Lead. London: Penguin Books Ltd, 2016.

16 Waldinger, Robert. "What Makes a Good Life? Lessons from the Longest Study on Happiness." Robert Waldinger: What makes a good life? Lessons from the longest study on happiness | TED Talk. November 2015. Accessed November 04, 2017. https://www.ted.com/talks/robert_waldinger_what_makes_a_good_life_lessons_from_the_longest_study_on_happiness.

17 Emerson, Ralph Waldo. The Essential Writings of Ralph Waldo Emerson (Modern Library Classics).

18 Brown, Brené, Ph. D., L.M.S.W. The Gifts of Imperfection: Let Go of Who You Think You're Supposed to Be and Embrace Who You Are. Center City, MN: Hazelden Publishing, 2010.

19 "The Most Motivational Talk EVER! - David Goggins | DRIVEN |." YouTube. June 22, 2017. Accessed November 04, 2017. https://www.youtube.com/watch?v=olrT1eHs1bo.

20 Frankl, Viktor E. and William J. Winslade. Man's Search for Meaning. Boston, MA: Beacon Press, 2006.

21 A Few Good Men. Directed by Rob Reiner. Performed by Tom Cruise, Demi Moore, Jack Nicholson. United States: Columbia Pictures, 1992. DVD.

22 Dostoyevsky, Fyodor, and Constance Garnett. *The Brothers Karamazov*. London: Heron Books, 1968.

23 Osbon, Diane K. ed. *Reflections on the Art of Living: A Joseph Campbell Companion*. New York: HarperCollins, 1991.

24 Roth, Eric. *The Curious Case of Benjamin Button*. Directed by David Fincher. Los Angeles: Paramount, 2008.

25 Macklemore, Ft. Skylar Grey. *Glorious*. Bendo, LLC. 2017.

26 Robbins, Tony. *Tony Robbins: I am Not Your Guru*. Directed by Joe Berlinger. U.S.A.: Netflix, 2016.

27 Brooks, David. *The Road to Character*. New York: Random House, 2016.

28 "Travis' 1836 Victory or Death Letter from the Alamo." Travis's 1836 Victory or Death Letter from the Alamo | TSLAC. June 02, 2017. Accessed November 04, 2017. https://www.tsl.texas.gov/travis-letter.

29 Overton, Patrick Miles. *The Leaning Tree*. Bloomington, MN: Bethany Press, 1975.

30 Campbell, Joseph and David Kudler. *Pathways to Bliss: Mythology and Personal Transformtion*. Novato, CA: New World Library, 2004.

31 Kahneman, Daniel, and Angus Deaton. "High Income Improves Evaluation of Life but Not Emotional Well-being." Proceedings of the National Academy of Sciences 107, No. 38 (September 21, 2010): 16489-6493. Accessed January 03, 2018. http://www.pnas.org/content/107/38/16489.

32 Tavernise, Sabrina. "U.S. Suicide Rate Surges to a 30-Year High." *The New York Times*. April 22, 2016. Accessed January 03, 2018. https://www.nytimes.com/2016/04/22/health/us-suicide-rate-surges-to-a-30-year-high.html.

33 Gallup Poll. "The State of the American Workplace." 2017: Gallup News. Accessed January 3, 2018. http://news.gallup.com/reports/199961/state-american-workplace-report-2017.aspx#

34 Kaste, Martin. "Haitians' Faith Unshaken By Earthquake." NPR. April 03, 2010. Accessed December 26, 2017. https://www.npr.org/templates/story/story.php?storyId=125477173.

35 Kremer, Gary R. *George Washington Carver: In His Own Words*. Columbia, MO: University of Missouri Press, 1987.

36 *When Harry Met Sally*. Directed by Rob Reiner. Performed by Billy Crystal, Meg Ryan. U.S.: MGM Home Entertainment, 2006. DVD.

37 Tzu, Lao, translated by Charles Johnson. *Tao Te Ching: Lao Tzu's Book of the Way and of Righteousness*. Kshetra Books.

38 "Thoughts On the Business of Life." *Forbes*. [Quote credited to Thomas A. Edison], Page 50, Column 1. New York: Forbes Inc. 1962 Februry 1.

39 Shakur, Tupac. *2Pacalypse Now*. Universal Music Enterprises 1241416332, 1991. CD.

40 King Jr., Martin Luther. *Strength to Love*. Minneapolis, MN: Fortress Press, 2010.

41 Macklemore, Ft. Skylar Grey. *Glorious*. Bendo, LLC. 2017.

42 Frankl, Viktor E. and William J. Winslade. *Man's Search for Meaning*. Boston, MA: Beacon Press, 2006.

43 "Rick – Opiod ADDICTION is in Our Own Backyard." Faces of Loudoun. Accessed October 23, 2017. http://endtheneed.org/2017/08/18/rick-opiod-addiction-is-in-our-own-backyard/.

44 "Network Transformation: Can Big Nonprofits Achieve Big Results?" The Bridgespan Group. Accessed January 03, 2018. https://www.bridgespan.org/insights/initiatives/transformative-scale/network-transformation-can-big-nonprofits-achieve.

45 George Bush: "Inaugural Address," January 20, 1989. Online by Gerhard Peters and John T. Woolley, The American Presidency Project. http://www.presidency.ucsb.edu/ws/?pid=16610.

46 Biema, David Van. "Mother Teresa's Crisis of Faith." *Time*, August 23, 2007. Accessed January 3, 2018. http://time.com/4126238/mother-teresas-crisis-of-faith/

47 Baldwin, James. *Sonny's Blues (Penguin 60s)*. London: Penguin Books, 1995.

48 Lewis, John, and Michael D'Orso. *Walking With the Wind: a Memoir of the Movement*. New York: Simon & Schuster Paperbacks, 2015.

49 Salam, Maya. "The Opioid Epidemic: A Crisis Years in the Making." *The New York Times*, October 26, 2017. Accessed January 3, 2018. https://www.nytimes.com/2017/10/26/us/opioid-crisis-public-health-emergency.html

50 Tavernise, Sabrina. "U.S. Suicide Rate Surges to a 30-Year High." *The New York Times*, April 22, 2016. Accessed Jan 3, 2018. https://www.nytimes.com/2016/04/22/health/us-suicide-rate-surges-to-a-30-year-high.html

51 Frankl, Viktor E. and William J. Winslade. *Man's Search for Meaning*. Boston, MA: Beacon Press, 2006.

52   Dianne Schilling, "10 Steps to Effective Listening," *Forbes*, November 9, 2012, https://www.forbes.com/sites/womensmedia/2012/11/09/10-steps-to-effective-listening/#763e36513891.

53   Patel, Vikram. "Mental Health for All by Involving All." Vikram Patel: Mental health for all by involving all | TED Talk. June 2012. Accessed October 27, 2017. https://www.ted.com/talks/vikram_patel_mental_health_for_all_by_involving_all/transcript#t-665984.

54   Singh, Maanvi. "The Friendship Bench Can Help Chase The Blues Away." NPR. January 10, 2017. Accessed January 03, 2018. https://www.npr.org/sections/goatsandsoda/2017/01/10/508588401/the-friendship-bench-can-help-chase-the-blues-away.

55   *Richard Evans' Quote Book*, 1971, Publisher's Press, ASIN: B000TV5WBW.

56   Frankl, Viktor E. and William J. Winslade. *Man's Search for Meaning*. Boston, MA: Beacon Press, 2006.

57   "Tecumseh – "Die Like a Hero Going Home." Native Heritage Project. November 17, 2013. Accessed January 03, 2018. https://nativeheritageproject.com/2013/11/17/tecumseh-die-like-a-hero-going-home/.

58   Henley, William Ernest. *A Book of Verses*. New York: Charles Scribner's Sons, 1893.